ALSO BY JOHN BAINES

In English:

The Stellar Man
The Science of Love
HypsoConsciousness
Morals for the 21st Century

Upcoming Titles:

The Development of the Inner World
Does Woman Exist?

In Spanish:

Los Brujos Hablan

Hipsoconciencia

El Hombre Estelar

La Ciencia Del Amor

Existe La Mujer?

El Desarrollo Del Mundo Interno

Depresion y Angustia: Como Neutralizarlas Usando Movimientos Corporales

Moral Para el siglo XXI

In German

Die Hexenmeister Sprechen

In Italian

La Scienza dell' Amore

Titles are also available in
Bulgarian, Russian, Latvian, and Portuguese

THE SECRET SCIENCE

BY

John Baines

Edited by the Editorial
Staff of the John Baines Institute, Inc.

2008
Published by

JOHN BAINES INSTITUTE, INC.

P.O. Box 8556 • F.D.R. Station • New York, NY • 10150
books@ihpny.org
www.ihpusa.org

THE SECRET SCIENCE

(Originally published as "Los Brujos Hablan")
By John Baines
Translated from Spanish by Evelyne Brown.
Formerly edited by Judith Hipskind.
(First Edition published by Llewellyn Publications
formerly, ISBN 0-87542-025-7)

ISBN 1-882692-01-2
Library of Congress Catalog Card Number: 93-91617

1st Edition 1980
2nd Edition 1994
3rd Edition 1998
4th Edition 2001
5th Edition 2004
6th Edition 2008
7th Edition 2012

Published by John Baines Institute, Inc.
Printed in the United States of America.
IHPBOOKS@gmail.com
www.ihpusa.org

THE SECRET SCIENCE

*Dedicated to sincere seekers of the truth
and to all those who yearn to free themselves
from error, ignorance, lies, and sorrow.*

Contents

Part One

Part Two

Practical Instructions
for Attaining Material and Spiritual Perfectioning

PREFACE

There are as many opinions and points of view as there are people. Each one defends "his truth," by using various arguments. Nevertheless, beyond truths, there is THE TRUTH.

What is truth? Truth is what is. It's the object by itself devoid of personal mirages. Truth can only be arrived at by developing the power to perceive and reason objectively, abandoning anthropocentrism which leads to the utterings of semi-sages. The world is full of semi-sages. True sages, similar to the sphinx, are silent, and only occasionally raise a corner of the veil.

This book does not seek to demonstrate any special theory or to broadcast mystical or religious principles of any kind, nor does it seek to dogmatize or enter into controversy on science or philosophy. It contains only the teachings of one Rosicrucian,* who

---

* The author is not referring to either the Rosicrucian Order (AMORC) or any other mundane group, but only to the esoteric tradition itself.

has personally verified everything that is stated herein, but one who is interested in addressing only those who have a genuine desire to improve themselves and to elevate themselves spiritually.

This book is written by one who knows and understands—in simple language within everyone's grasp. It is addressed to all those who have eyes to see and ears to hear; and to those who are not in agreement with scientific, philosophical and social conventionalisms; to those who sense that "all is not well" with the human species; to those who suffer and cannot explain their pain; to those who feel a private and sensitive chord touched upon reading this book; to those who want to know the truth of life practically and personally; to those who feel misunderstood by the world and its people; to those whose ideal is a better world through spiritual elevation of the individual; to those who abhor injustice, misery, and ignorance; and to all those who yearn to better themselves mentally and spiritually.

This book teaches some of the rudiments of Rosicrucian Occultism. The genuine Rosicrucian Order, which exists as such only in secret, is the heir and depository of a science which permits the achievement of voluntary mutations in the human beast in order to transform it into a HUMAN BEING WHO IS CONSCIOUS OF AND RESPONSIBLE FOR HIS TRUE ROLE AS A CHILD OF GOD.

It is the depository of the great mystery of human duality which is the following:

THE HUMAN RACE HAS TWO DIFFERENT ORIGINS, ONE ANIMAL-TERRESTRIAL AND ANOTHER, HUMAN-EXTRATERRESTRIAL.

In ancient times, extraterrestrial men visited our planet who were physically the same as we are, but otherwise extraordinarily evolved. During their lengthy evolution these men had achieved the permanent incorporation within themselves of many of the qualities of the Great Architect and Sublime Alchemist of the Universe. Their consciousness had reached such exhalted levels that for us they would be gods.

These beings left descendants on our planet who imperceptibly intermingled with the rest of humanity. These descendants carry dormant in their genes capabilities inherited from those beings. Rosicrucians are direct descendants of that exalted race; they are the priests or depositories of all their science. Other descendants who have not been initiated have formed the elite of the world as geniuses, philosophers, reformers, artists, etc.

These "children of the stars" are the true and authentic MEN, as opposed to the HUMANIZED ANIMALS of terrestrial origin.

This duality of the species explains its endless anomalies and contradictions. It gives us much to think about and explains the mythical origin of the gods which comes down to us from remotest antiquity. It unveils the mystery of Jesus Christ, the story of Cain and Abel, child prodigies, extrasensory perception, etc.

Animal-terrestrial humanity has always feared, respected and hated those who came from beyond. They instinctively sense something strange and unknown in them. They see on their brows the divine sign and recognize their superiority. The great struggles of humanity show us this conflict between animal darkness and divine light. *Homo sapiens* struggle between two contradictory feelings with respect to extraterrestrial beings: hate and love. Generally *homo sapiens* crucify the extraterrestrials during life only to adore them after their death, in the same way as a madman who kills his benefactor. These MEN have fought and continue to fight tenaciously to raise the level of humanity, while the beast, thirsty for blood, constantly seeks a propitious victim on whom to vent its fury and it therefore feeds itself on the likes of a Jacob of Molay, a Christ, a Gandhi, or a Kennedy.

The Rosicrucian Order will initiate any citizen of a high moral character and an authentic spirit of self-improvement into THE GREAT MYSTERY OF THE TRANSFORMATION OF THE HUMANIZED ANIMAL INTO A MAN.

Their work is secret, since they must avoid attacks from beasts disguised as Men.

Very few are aware of the true objective of life, of what is really worthwhile and of what it is to know oneself and to find oneself so that some day it will be possible to face oneself and say, "this is what I am."

Human beings search for the truth by means of complicated theories and they saturate themselves with tons and tons of knowledge, from which they only acquire a veneer of culture and education, while within their souls still remaining as much of an animal as the caveman. They do not realize that the only place where everything can be found is within their own interior. They ignore the fact that the greatest truths and secrets of life are found in the simplest things and never in complicated, twisted or refined ones. They do not realize that there is more science, more humanity, truth and beauty in a single human teardrop than can be found in all the universities of the world.

Only one who knows himself can succeed in gradually separating himself from the animal realm.

Rosicrucian science in its vulgar, fragmentary and minimal expression is known as Occultism.

Those who smile skeptically at the word, Occultism, ignore the fact that it represents only a small part of its exoteric aspect which has filtered through to common knowledge. True knowledge is found on the esoteric side and has never been revealed to the world, and can only be accessed through real Rosicrucian initiation.

This book may be the gateway to a new life for many that is infinitely more exalted and human.

The Gospel of St. Matthew, Chapter 7, Numbers 13 and 14 says:

"Enter ye by the narrow gate; for wide is the gate and broad is the way that leadeth to destruction, and many there be that enter thereat."

"For narrow is the gate and straitened is the way, that leadeth unto life, and few there be that find it."

John Baines

AN INTRODUCTION TO HERMETICISM

Hermetic Philosophy is the Mother Science from which all knowledge originates, since its fundamental principles are the laws of life and Nature before which the alternatives of doubt and faith do not exist.

Hermetic Philosophy is neither theoretical nor abstract, but is a science that is absolutely verifiable, nor is it an invention of any particular person, even though it was disseminated by Hermes Trismegistus, the great sage, who according to tradition, lived 15,000 years ago.

Hermeticism is the faithful description of natural laws that govern the existence of human beings, the planet Earth and the entire Universe. Hermeticism is not a political movement; it is not a religion; it is not an esoteric sect, nor is it an academy of traditional knowledge. It is a science which teaches the art of living wisely in accordance with natural laws that govern our existence, with the purpose of achieving inner peace and a harmonious relationship with our fellowman. Hermetic Philosophy instructs man to consciously accept a humanistic attitude within society, overcoming egoism, hate, incomprehension and fanaticism.

The application of this Philosophy leads to the development of the higher faculties of the human being, so that each individual can be a conscious collaborator in the formation of a new world that is more human, more just and with greater opportunities for all. This is achieved through the creation of a state of cerebral consciousness that is more elevated than the average one and which permits the development of little-known latent faculties, achieving a state of higher understanding and the acceptance of higher ethical and moral values. This transformation is equivalent to a process of internal maturation which converts the individual into a being duly prepared for having success in life.

SOME PRINCIPLES OF HERMETICISM

COMPREHENSION: The Hermetic Philosopher has no dogmas. He does not accept truth on faith. He receives Teachings, reflects on them, and after comprehending them, proves them for himself in daily life. He is open to all possibilities and carefully chooses the steps to follow in his life, making sure to always apply what he has learned, since one of the main characteristics of Hermetic Philosophy is its practical and operative character. Each philosopher must be responsibly practical and precise in his own search for which Hermeticism offers the tools and the keys necessary to achieve complete fulfillment as a human being.

TRUTH: The Hermetic Philosopher must be an eternal seeker of truth. It is necessary to differentiate between two truths; the ultimate truth which is the one that is beyond appearances and the common or semi-truth. The ultimate truth is the Truth that has always existed and that will always exist, which corresponds to the expression of the laws of Nature that govern the existence of the entire Universe.

In order to succeed in deciphering this Truth, it is necessary to become a Sage. The main difficulty in doing this resides in the multiple semi-truths, which in general, are circumstantial. They might be true today and stop being so tomorrow. They might be true for some and false for others since they are subject to points of view which are limited by cultural, historical or ideological differences.

SUCCESS: It is the achievement of one's own aspirations which are as much material as they are spiritual. It is connected to the profound comprehension of what one wants to obtain through perseverance, order, the level of internal commitment, the absence of contradictions, will power and the lack of vices.

LIBERTY: It is the inner capacity that the individual has for choosing and directing his life towards higher values, overcoming the blind mandates of passion and negative external influences. The only true liberty does not depend on external conditions, but rather is an inner condition in which the individual can exercise his higher will, free from all compulsions or alienations. In general the concept of liberty is commonly interpreted as "libertinism" which is the mechanical and blind expression of basic appetites. This mistaken concept can be dangerous for the well-being of the community and for an entire country.

DISCIPLINE: It is the personal capacity for postponing the pleasure of the moment for the benefit of a greater and more important objective.

WILL POWER: It is the basic tool for being able to achieve what one desires, overcoming existing obstacles. To have will power does not consist in "doing what one wants," but rather in "doing what one does not want," but which is necessary to accomplish because it is the correct and adequate thing to do. Will power can be developed just like muscles. It is the power that opens the path for personal development and material and spiritual success.

WORK: Work is something sacred for the Hermeticist, since it permits him to temper his character and ennoble himself as a human being. Work liberates a person from useless idleness which normally is the source of all vices. Work is the means for enriching a country. All work dignifies and is the only legitimate source of wealth. The concept of "gratis" does not exist in Nature which is why the success of a person is directly related to his capacity for effort and work.

CAPITAL: For the Hermetic Philosopher, true capital is not money, but is the inner wealth that exists within each person. This wealth is inexhaustible and is the capacity "to create" that the human being has. When the Hermetic Philosopher puts into practice the knowledge he acquires and succeeds in adequately disciplining his body and his mind, he has direct access to this inexhaustible source. He will thus be able to materialize his ideas, desires and projects in a real way, as long as he has managed to overcome the blind egoism that compels him to not respect the rights of his fellowman.

HOMELAND: It is the implementation of higher qualities at an individual level which transforms each person into one of the most valuable assets for a country. A great and powerful country can only build itself through the union of citizens, proud of their homeland, and who contribute the best of themselves for the enrichment and benefit of all.

ESPRIT DE CORPS: A person by himself is a body; a family is a body; a country is a body and also, the entire Universe is a body.

This is a truth on which the student of Hermeticism must profoundly reflect since the entire Universe is submitted to the corporative system.

In all bodies, there exists a basic law which says, "one for all, and all for one."

All the great feats that have been carried out by mankind have been accomplished under this power. It is necessary to analyze the structure of one's own physical body in order to understand that biologically speaking, it is not a solid unit, but rather corresponds to an assembly of associated systems which are: the respiratory system, the circulatory system, the digestive system and the procreative system. The harmonious working together of these apparatuses is what guarantees health and life. The same thing happens at the level of one's own mind. Mental health is synonymous with unified integrated thought under the direction of a strong and mature "I."

The great evils of humanity come from the breaking of the corporative system. Each person seeks to do what he desires or wants without stopping to think of the common good, thus producing disunion and chaos. The common good and personal well-being must be balanced so that neither one of them harms the liberty of the other.

Hermeticism is a knowledge that if taken with responsibility and a higher perspective by the student, will bring him very positive concrete changes in his life, providing him a personal satisfaction that he never before experienced. He will learn to enjoy the truth and will be able to extract the profound meaning from the daily experiences of his life.

He will be able to convert himself into a real sage and a real winner.

Transcending oneself. This is the key of Hermeticism.

PART ONE

CHAPTER I

WHAT IS OCCULTISM?

During recent years the advance in science and technology has been incredible. New and revolutionary concepts have emerged in all fields of human activity. Today more is known about physics, chemistry, surgery, disease, and other fields than ever before. In the not too distant future, human beings will even be able to move to other planets.

Despite all this, man himself has not changed at all. His brain still works in the same way as it did two thousand years before Christ; his fears, hatreds, passions and anxieties are the same. The conquest of the inner world has been non-existent. Much is known about the secrets of matter and energy, but nothing is known about the mind or the force which maintains life. Very few can state with certainty, "I know myself."

Nevertheless, this does not seem to worry the

great human mass made arrogant by the apparent power of man over Nature.

Only illness, misfortune and death occasionally intervene to teach humility, and then man who arrogantly believes himself to be master and lord of the universe, bows his head, just as crushed and impotent as primitive man was before the fury of the elements.

Only in those moments does he meditate on life and ask himself: "What is life?" "Why is God so unjust?" "Who am I?" "Where do I come from?" "Where am I going?" "Why do we all have to die?" "Is there no happiness?"

Some, who are too materialistic or too lazy to think, content themselves with attributing everything to chance.

Religions endeavor by all the means available to offer comfort through different dogmas which they attribute to divine origin. Nevertheless, scientific laws are implacably logical and powerful, making it difficult to reconcile them with religious dogmas which appeal only to faith.

Deep inside himself, man lives confused and fearful of the morrow. In order to alleviate this confusion and anguish which arise from a vision of a world that is apparently chaotic, unjust, and governed by chance, he surrounds himself with materialistic progress, luxury and amusement.

Through social life, parties and friendships he tries to forget his spiritual emptiness and close his eyes to the terrible spectacle of life.

In the midst of this chaos there exists a Secret Society which has maintained for thousands of years in its original purity, a science which allows individuals access to a new and higher conscious awareness, through which they are able to know themselves, become aware of the mystery of life and truth and bring to life their latent mental capacities. This Secret Society is the ORDER OF HERMETIC ROSICRUCIANS. This fraternity preserves in its secret files a science which comes from the farthest reaches of antiquity, and which was communicated to humanity by extraterrestrial visitors. This science is Occultism, whose true teachings are kept secret, with only personal interpretations having reached common people from those who have been able to glimpse a minute portion of these secrets. This knowledge has been kept hidden due to the fact that only those individuals who are willing to study seriously and who have acquired a certain degree of spiritual evolution may have access to it. This is similar to the law which reserves certain rights only for those over 21 years of age.

There exists a mistaken concept that the human being is an intelligent organism which is completely and totally evolved. Nevertheless, man is still only on the threshold of his mental development. Throughout the ages there have been men who have achieved a more complete development than the rest, men who were illuminated and inspired by Rosicrucian science, which formerly had its center of action in Egypt, having been started there by its founder, Hermes Trismegistus.

Some of these men had names like Pythagoras, Socrates, Plato, Jesus, Orpheus, Dante, Descartes, Franklin, Edison, Newton and Bacon. They, and many others, have formed a true spiritual aristocracy, infinitely more important than any social or financial aristocracy.

Rosicrucians appear and disappear throughout the history of mankind, according to certain preordained cycles. They were especially well-known between the fifteenth and seventeenth centuries, winning fame as magicians, sages and alchemists, but disappeared soon afterwards to work in secret for the welfare of humanity, maintaining only certain vanguards who taught Rosicrucian science to those whose conscious state made them worthy of instruction.

Unfortunately, some individuals who have only had a passing contact with an authentic Rosicrucian have founded institutions for purely commercial purposes, which they have labeled Rosicrucian. These usurpers have tried to prove their legitimacy with bundles of documents in which they are supposedly recognized as the "only true Rosicrucians." However, they have forgotten that by tradition, the real Rosicrucian never reveals himself by means of documents, signs or words, but rather by his knowledge and deeds, by his way of being, by his manner of speaking and acting. In spite of the fact that these pseudo-Rosicrucian organizations have had no contact with those authentic Rosicrucians from the fifteenth century, they have played a useful role in awakening the interest of the average person in these studies.

Just as there are primary, secondary and university levels in the field of education, there is also a comparable progression in true Rosicrucian studies. Only in an organization where an individual is truly and not symbolically initiated will he find the highest teaching. "Many are called, but few are chosen" takes on special meaning here. Many have sought the light of occultism in various and sundry organizations, but few have found the true institution where there really is light and truth, since only the one guided by his own spirit can find it.

In spite of the abundance of centers of learning, in no part of the world, in no school, and in no university is the individual taught to live. Rare are the beings who can affirm with complete exactness that they know how to live, since it is not intelligence, culture or titles which teach the individual this art. Paradoxically, sometimes those who are most cultured in appearance are woefully ignorant because the most terrible ignorance is ignorance of oneself, ignorance of the mystery of life, ignorance of the arcanum of Our Father or Creator whom we call God. It is the ignorance of the mystery of death, ignorance of love, kindness, beauty and true wisdom, the ignorance of brotherhood and of the bond between all the peoples of the world.

We live in an age in which, despite the great number of Christians that there are in the world, Christ's teaching, "love one another," is daily trampled in the dust. The law of "might is right" rules and the most bestial egoism has been converted into a shield and buckler for man, whose greatest desire is to gain as much money as possible, in order to enjoy the power that riches buy.

Only in the face of death is the idea of God, love, and spirit reborn.

There exists a desperate search for happiness through material pleasures which strongly stimulate the senses and offer a type of sensual euphoria. In spite of the dominion science has achieved over matter, the individual has moved towards a diametrically opposite attitude: he has become a slave to his material possessions. How many, for example, work very hard in order to maintain a luxury car? How many lose their decency and human dignity, debasing themselves for gold, becoming intoxicated, or profiting by another's misfortune?

The one who lives attached to material pleasure enjoys a sensual euphoria which makes him incapable of seeing how much he has lost his human qualities.

Material objects hypnotize and devour just like the boa constrictor which entrances a bird before swallowing it.

Nevertheless, in this era of tremendous materialism there are privileged beings who yearn to know the mysteries of life, conquer destiny, promote love and brotherhood among human beings, free the world from evil, mold their characters to overcome vice, complexes, weakness, etc. There are many, who, having suffered excessively or having been born awakened and conscious, desperately seek the light of knowledge which can lead them to find themselves in order to achieve everything they desire in life.

Some wish to know why "bad luck" always seems to follow them; others have not attained happiness in love or cannot triumph in life because of shyness or a lack of personality. There are some who suffer from incurable nervous or mental disorders, or other ailments and who can learn to overcome them or to alleviate their effects by the correct use of the mind. Those misunderstood by their families, orphans of love, those who suffer spiritual abandonment, sorrow or deception, can free themselves and be victorious.

Those who have problems of any kind, terrible as they may seem, should not despair. *Occultism is the ultimate and sacred science which teaches how to live wisely by correctly using the forces of Nature.*

Occultism is the study of man and the laws of

Nature, and the way in which these act and influence human beings. It is called occultism because it is truly a science that is "occult" (in the sense of hidden) from passionate, selfish or vengeful beings, or from those who are slaves to their material desires.

The word, occultism, immediately produces a negative reaction among listeners because occultism has become a synonym for "magic," "witchcraft," "demonology," "satanism," etc. The fantastic and copious literature on these subjects, all jumbled together under the classification of "occult sciences," has greatly contributed to this idea. The majority of these books have been written by vain individuals who have never had any contact with true and sacred occultism, who have only studied fragments of esotericism from other equally fantastic and unrealistic books. Charlatanism and occultism have become synonymous in people's minds. Pseudo-occultists beneath a mask of grandiloquency and theatricality have claimed magical powers, clairvoyance and the ability to recall their past lives or previous incarnations, generally identifying themselves as some famous person of bygone ages.

Similarly, much publicity has been given to occult phenomena witnessed by Europeans in India and Tibet, which is why all those interested in occult sciences look towards those countries hoping to find there what they have not been able to find in their native country. They naively think they can spend twelve hours a day in astral projection, "contemplating their navel" or meditating. They think that this is the most perfect condition to which human beings can aspire. They do not realize that the complicated gymnastics called Yoga, for example, are only a means to an end, which the Westerner can achieve more easily by other methods more in accordance with his strength, activity or vigor, in order not to fall into Hindu passiveness and apathy. There is a notable difference between the Eastern and Western constitution, and therefore it is not wise for the people of the West to adopt Hindu practices which may lead to the disintegration of their personality.

There are currently many organizations of a philosophical nature which do much good, but which are far from leading the aspirant to true communion with Isis and to the knowledge of Nature's secrets. Out of one thousand schools of occultism, there is perhaps one where the aspirant will find the light of true knowledge and receive a true initiation. The rest are only centers of study where theoretical information is provided; not knowledge, and wisdom, even less.

The prime objective of occultism is the liberation of the human being; liberation from ignorance, pain, bestiality, lies, destiny and death, in order to some day change the world and create a new world of conscious men entirely responsible for their human quality.

Many set out on this road to excellence with great enthusiasm, but believe that just three or four prayers, meditations, or incantations are sufficient in order to receive all types of power and knowledge by divine grace. It is necessary to be realistic, since everything in life costs something. Occultism is a science which requires dedication, tenacity and constant study and practice, since it is a science which involves nothing less than the comprehension and knowledge of God, man and life. A great majority of people lose their enthusiasm because they study for one or two years and want to get everything in that short period of time.

The person who obtains a degree as a doctor has to study approximately twenty years of his life, yet some people want to decipher the mystery of life in two or three years. Only with limitless tenacity, valor and confidence in oneself at all costs, can one attain great achievements. Undoubtedly, those who only wish to change their character, strengthen their personality or attain some material success, will not need to push themselves as much as those who desire a union with their own spirit.

Those who study out of curiosity will regrettably lose their time and run the risk of endangering their lives because contact with the flame of truth may burn those whose souls have not been purified of selfishness and human passion.

Different sects and schools study and utilize some aspects of occultism, generally under other names. Examples of these are Masonry, Martinism,

Yoga and absolutely all religions. Anyone who knows something about occultism will realize that religious institutions are true secret societies and that is why all religions have taken various symbols for their rites from those of occult fraternities of bygone ages. For example, in the Catholic religion, Isis is transformed into the Virgin Mary; the Ankh into the Catholic cross; the wand of Anubis into the bishop's crosier, and the ceremonies of ritual invocation become the Mass, etc.

These movements have knowledge of only a small part of this science, a knowledge which is generally used for their own exclusive benefit. This is the case with some religions that treat their followers like sheep, keeping them unaware of the real meaning of the symbols and rituals, with the priests stating that these are "mysteries."

At a much higher level is Masonry whose philosophy and symbols are entirely Rosicrucian. This great institution merits our deepest respect and has cooperated to a great extent with the accomplishment of the Rosicrucian ideals of liberty, equality and fraternity. Unfortunately, Masonry has lost many of the keys to hermetic science, and at present their initiation is purely symbolic.

In ancient Egypt the study of occultism was the privilege of priests and pharaohs. That is where Hermes Trismegistus appeared, known as the Father of Modern Occultism, who summarized Rosicrucian wisdom under seven principles, known as The Seven

Hermetic Principles, which are the basis of occultism and the key to all phenomena. These are: Mind, Correspondence, Vibration, Polarity, Rhythm, Cause and Effect, and Generation.

Mind: "All is mind, everything is energy." "The Universe is mental."

Correspondence: "As it is above, so it is below; as it is below, so it is above."

Vibration: "Nothing is stationary; everything vibrates."

Polarity: "Everything is double. Everything has its opposite. Extremes meet."

Rhythm: "All is ebb and flow, action and reaction, advance and recoil."

Cause and Effect: "Nothing happens by chance. Everything happens according to the law."

Generation: "Generation is manifest in everything. Everything is masculine and feminine."

The careful study of these principles is a true master key for opening the doors to all knowledge.

Nature hides in her bosom the greatest secrets of life and the one who, following the teachings of Christ, "becomes like a child," can read in her like an open book.

The requirements for meriting the teaching of this science are: to have an impersonal ideal for the benefit of humanity; to practice love, fraternity and equality with all human beings regardless of class, race or color; to strongly desire to excel morally and spiritually and to attain mastery over passion.

If you wish to excel, listen attentively to the voice of occult teaching:

"Nothing will be denied you if you understand, practice and accomplish the divine science of true occultism which enables man to consciously identify himself with the divine principle that he carries within."

This book is meant only as a small ray of light in the darkness of the world, a ray which shows the way to whomsoever wishes to find the light of truth within his own spirit. "Know thyself" must be our motto and the entrance way to the temple of wisdom.

CHAPTER II

Man

Homo Sapiens, the fickle, contradictory and passionate creature, incorporates the most diverse and varied tendencies. One moment, he reaches the utmost heights of kindness, love and sacrifice and in another, he sinks to the lowest depths of bestiality and evil. The human being is man and beast at the same time and between these two inclinations of bestiality and divinity, his "I" hovers in permanent and continuous fluctuation.

From this duality, arises a need to establish a new scale for human classification, one that is beyond intelligence, titles, political power or wealth. This classification has to do with the distance of man, be it nearer or further from his animal condition. Intelligence or a man's social, cultural and financial status tell us nothing about the human quality of an individual. A scientist, a nobleman or a brilliant politician may be nearer to the animal condition than an uneducated person. *Consciousness is what determines this difference in human status.* The more conscious an individual, the further he is from the animal condition and vice versa. The level of consciousness is determined by the capacity of man to exist and act free from psychic automatisms. The mind can only function correctly when it is free from emotional disturbances, instinctive compulsions, and all that distorts and clouds its thoughts. We could say that consciousness is that "I" which governs the mind.

However, it is possible to find an intelligent person who is unconscious, since intelligence and consciousness are two different things.

Because physical phenomena can be measured, classified and evaluated, certain laws can be established. This does not occur with mental phenomena, since we are only aware of the "conscious" mind which is but a small part of the whole. When it comes to the subconscious mind, we are almost completely in the dark. It is a well-known fact that the subconscious mind is gullible and malleable and lacks the capacity for judgment. How does one determine when an individual is thinking with his subconscious or conscious mind? It is obvious to assume that if oneiric or subconscious states have been the basis for reasoning, then this reasoning will lack credibility. Ignorance of precise mental processes has lead us to doubt that they are efficient. It has also lead us to not recognize that perception can be seriously damaged due to factors that we are not aware of. Imagine if someone affirmed that all human beings are, and have always been insane. What concrete means do we have to refute this? What points of reference do we have? Is it possible that the human mental state is imperfect? That the mind has lost, or lacks certain essential qualities for its complete and perfect functioning? Therefore, the difficulty of studying and proving this phenomenon is evident, because it would only be possible to do so by first acquiring the very qualities that are lacking.

Rosicrucian Philosophy states that certain essential capacities of the human mind have atrophied which are, however, capable of being acquired through Rosicrucian practices. The former statement amply explains and justifies the enormous range of anomalies in human behavior.

Genuine Rosicrucians are the direct heirs of extraordinarily evolved extraterrestrial visitors who taught them the total development of the mind. Pseudo-Rosicrucians are those who study and profess certain disciplines to strengthen the will, educate the character and achieve the perception of certain extrasensorial phenomena. Nevertheless, after undertaking all these practices, they still lack the qualities which we consider to be atrophied in the human mind.

In spite of this, all the mystery of mysteries is hidden within man because he is the son of God, and is essentially made in His image. He is a chained god within whom there is divine power and wisdom, but he does not know how to use it, because he is bound to matter. He is a slave of everything that be it pleasant or unpleasant, reaches him through his senses.

States such as the desire for comfort, greed, gluttony, arrogance, covetousness, vanity and a thousand other passional states, are those which govern as lord and master, this microcosm which we call "man."

The "I," which should be the master of the individual, is displaced by various desires and psychic and instinctive states which take possession of, and govern, the complex machinery which is the body, or the vehicle of the soul. Man does not have only one "I," but thousands of different "I's" which follow one after the other like a kaleidoscope, constantly changing its design. Each one of these "I's" usurps the throne or scepter which belongs to the legitimate and authentic "I." This divine "I" is like a king constantly being dethroned and imprisoned by his subjects.

One who has felt a sort of inner pain of being alive, has felt at that moment, the suffering of the "I" which is constantly being displaced as the director of its microcosm. We can compare man to a mansion full of servants who fruitlessly await a master who never arrives. Each one of these servants endeavors to usurp the throne until he in turn is displaced by one stronger than he who will also, in turn, be expelled.

This is the terrible emptiness or weariness of life which is so common in our time. It is the "I" that suffers intensely and does not want to continue living under such adverse conditions. If this situation continues for too long, the "I" or soul may leave the body, transforming the individual into the living dead, because only the remaining animal or instinctive condition will maintain life within his body. Man, contrary to popular opinion, has none of those qualities which we call consciousness, personality, liberty or free will, since all his decisions are the product of automatisms or external influences. Life, for him, passes in a twilight state of sopor caused by this constant changing of "I's." We are all fully aware of what hypnotism means, but we have never really considered that it can be practiced collectively and simultaneously on all humanity by the planetary forces that seek their own benefit at the expense of human self-determination. These planetary forces endeavor to keep humanity asleep so that it never sees truth and reality. From birth until death, the individual lives in the deepest of sleeps and everything that happens to him is "dreamt." He believes he is awake; but he is only dreaming. He believes he is free; but he is only dreaming of freedom. He believes he has a will of his own, but only dreams it is so.

Consciousness does not exist for the common man since he is a perfect, complete machine. Only when man recognizes his mechanical state is there a possibility of his obtaining freedom, will and consciousness. Man does nothing under his own initiative; everything simply "happens," just like the rain, the rising of the sun, the whirling or calming of the wind. He reacts exactly like a machine in all circumstances, and upon receiving an initial stimulus, he carries out a work which was previously known and programmed in him.

The reaction of the individual at all times is dictated by the recording of impressions, experiences and knowledge which are carried in his brain cells and which constitute a sort of magnetic tape that governs his conduct. This recording has been made by influences outside the individual, so that his personality, which is the assembly of cellular recordings, constitutes something like a projection of society's values.

Each individual is a true "android" produced by his parents, circumstances, environment, education and the influence of other minds. This android, like a good robot, can only operate by combining data or circuits which have been implanted in it by these external influences. His "I" is entirely obliterated and is unable to act in the midst of this entanglement of circuits. His reactions are therefore dictated by other minds and forces unknown to him. *Can he therefore consider himself free and with a will of his own?* We could say that a child is like a blank record or magnetic tape upon which are recorded or collected all the impressions, knowledge, emotions and desires he experiences. The quality of this recording determines his destiny, since he can only use that which was recorded in his mind. He analyzes everything according to this scale of values and because of this, it would be impossible for him to know the truth. All human misfortunes and problems arise from an unfortunate mental recording. Occultism teaches how to change all this, beginning by gradually erasing everything negative from the tape in order to replace it with a positive recording. The psychiatrist is unable to penetrate deeply enough into the psyche of the individual because he is unaware of the secrets of the mind. Only by delving into the deepest strata of the subconscious, is it possible to bring to light, in all their clarity, childhood experiences and the impressions received while within the mother's womb. Occultism holds the means of complete psychical penetration and can totally change the destiny and life of an individual causing a true "mutation." Of course, in a book published for the man in the street, this method cannot be revealed since it could be a terrible weapon in the wrong hands. We can only say that by means of the proper manipulation of certain forces, it is possible to provoke a complete opening of the subconscious, just like the splitting open of an orange to see what there is inside.

CHAPTER III

THE SPIRIT AND THE SOUL

There is great confusion as to what the "soul" and the "spirit" are. They are generally considered to be synonymous. Rosicrucian Philosophy says that "man is a spirit which inhabits a body and man has a soul. Spirit he is, soul he has." The spirit is the divine, immortal and eternal part, the divine spark or emanation from God which we carry in the deepest recesses of our being. This is the strength of God, the eternal and unquenchable light which illuminates us at crucial moments in our lives. We could compare God to a large body of water which vertiginously sprays millions of drops of water, each one, equivalent to the spirit of an individual human being. Therefore, man is a spirit incarnated in a body.

The soul is the intelligent animal part, or rather that which we call personality which forms gradually as a result of the spirit-body union. When a person is sad or suffers a state of profound depression, it is generally the soul which feels this. On the other hand, when someone says, "I am who I am," it is the spirit who is manifesting itself.

Man's ultimate goal consists of achieving the marriage between the soul and spirit. To this end it is necessary to cultivate the soul, giving it consciousness and intelligence. The soul is like a young animal or small child upon whom we must impose our will, to teach obedience at all times, rather than the reverse, which would mean to be guided by the animal part.

When the soul acquires consciousness and intelligence, we can act at will with the forces of Nature.

The Hermetic law of Correspondence states: "As it is above, so it is below; as it is below, so it is above." Applying this to man, the microcosm, we can affirm that all that is within us is also outside of us and therefore, he who conquers his internal nature is also able to achieve dominion over the external.

Alchemy, the traditional art of Occultism, teaches how to transmute base metals into gold. In the spiritual sense, this symbolizes the transmutation of base passions into virtues. The soul, which sheds the dross of unbridled emotions and passions, is like a shining golden shield which protects the human being from evil and misery.

As a manifestation of the soul we can appreciate

the characteristic stamp that the familiar collective soul impresses on all its members. Its features not only produce a physical resemblance, but there is also what we call "a familial likeness," something that can be sensed when meeting one of its members. This collective soul can in some cases turn into a selfish and passionate tyrant, which brings disgrace and misery to the members of the group. If there is harmony and perfect union, it can bring prosperity, protection, wealth and happiness.

It is interesting to observe the soul of a country from this collective point of view. All its inhabitants have similar idiosyncrasies and a particular type of behavior which do not arise from communal life. All foreigners or outsiders arriving there are quickly absorbed into this collective force and they soon adopt the regional air until they become like the native inhabitants. Towards this collective soul are drawn all the individual's emotions, instincts, thoughts and passions and because of this, for one to succeed in any way or to overcome mediocrity, it would be necessary to elevate oneself above the vibration of the collective soul by submitting oneself to a strict personal discipline.

Just as the human being has a soul, so do animals, plants and even minerals, since there is life in everything. As the Hermetic Principle of Vibration declares: "Nothing is stationary, everything vibrates."

In speaking of the soul, we should consider the

heart as the center of all psychic and emotional life. Great praise has been raised in its honor and it is considered wise to act upon its dictates. In truth, the heart when not correctly educated, is the great enemy of the human being because it constantly drives him to make mistakes. The heart is like the soul of a child; it immediately attracts any vibration or force which has the power to drive the individual to commit acts which he will subsequently regret. The invisible world that surrounds us is a receptacle which retains good and bad vibrations.   In expansive moments, these vibrations are attracted to and are taken in by the heart as its own. Afterwards, the mind suffers serious disturbances as a result of these emotional states. Thus it can be seen that love, as well as hate, is blind. For example, a man in love will lose and sacrifice everything for the woman he loves, and the man who hates, carries within himself the seed of his own destruction.

Love must at all times be governed by reason for it to be a positive force for the individual. Otherwise, it is a force as blind as hate. Of course, it is infinitely better for man to love than hate, but it is necessary to know how to love; to love impersonally without egoism. How few know true love! A woman falls in love and therefore believes that she loves. Usually, this supposed love is a deception by the heart. It is an intoxication of psychic magnetism that produces a particular kind of euphoria which has been called love. When the desire for possession is satisfied and the intoxication is over, this false love ends. This is the most common cause of failed marriages. A man and woman marry, very much in love, and discover after a time that they are only joined by habit and legal contract. This is very natural, since human passions are much like the wind that blows and then subsides. Only love which is born from the perfect union of the heart and brain can be called real. This love is immortal and eternal because it is within the vibrational field of the spirit, and everything spiritual is sacred, divine, eternal and immortal.

The key to many secrets can be found hidden between the lines of what has been said above. One who can read and understand can make use of these secrets. Wisdom itself cannot be communicated; only basic facts can be presented for the purpose of study and practice.

CHAPTER IV

THE MIND

The mind is man's magic wand. It is the marvelous toy with which it is possible to travel millions of miles per second to the farthest planet, since distance and time are nonexistent for it. The mind is a kind of fantastic magic hat from which we can extract everything.

Another Hermetic principles states: "All is Mind; the Universe is Mental."

Only upon understanding that everything that exists in the material sense is only mental energy whose vibratory wavelength has decreased until it becomes solid, can we then understand the importance of studying and educating the mind.

The brain is similar to a radio transmitter which constantly sends out and receives radio waves. Of course, thought waves are much more subtle and powerful. All thought is electro-magnetic energy of a high vibration. The brain is a powerful generator of energy, whose vibratory wavelength depends upon the degree of culture and intellectual development of the individual. Therefore, it is very difficult for a man who has a long mental wave to understand another with a short mental wave. This is the reason behind those unending discussions which arise between two people who believe the same thing, but who do not understand each other because they have different vibrations.

The mind is the doorway to what is known as the fourth dimension or plane of energy. Everything that can be imagined by man is a reality on the plane of energy and therefore can be accomplished in the material realm. Upon thinking, an emission of electro-magnetic energy is produced which gives rise to a being possessing a certain degree of consciousness who will live on that energetic level. This being will have a consciousness in relation to the individual's mental and psychic state at the moment it is generated and it will become a true offspring or child. All our habitual thoughts are mental offspring, and as children do, they must nourish themselves from their parents. Accordingly, we can understand the truth of the aphorism which says, "as a man thinketh, so shall he be."

These mental children are the ones who will decide the future destiny of an individual, bringing him "good or bad luck" in accordance with his vibratory quality. Sometimes upon meeting a person, we experience a great sadness or depressive state. This is due to the fact that we have attracted his vibratory group of mental children which in this example, are of a negative character. With other people, we feel happy and confident and they raise our spirits. It is vitally important to carefully select our friends, always avoiding those who possess negative irradiations of a pessimistic or fatalistic character, since all meetings or conversations produce an interchange of magnetism and mental matter. On the mental plane all thought is material and is as concrete as a stone or a chair in the physical world. If we could see into the mental plane we would perceive each individual surrounded by mental forms in accordance with their particular or dominant vibration. With a passionate or highly instinctive individual, we would see tigers, bulls, hyenas, etc. An individual full of love towards others, will constantly emit thoughts in the form of beautiful flowers and plants. On the other hand, a miser will resemble an octopus with many tentacles. Another individual, closed to all new ideas, will have the shape of a cube.

If an individual could at any given moment concentrate all his mental energy on one single aim, he could achieve miracles. In reality, we see that our minds jump dizzily from one thought to another during the day, and there is no rest even during sleep at night. This continuous wandering gives rise to a fantastic waste of energy, yielding in the individual a state of scattered energy. To achieve a better life, we must gain dominion over the imagination so as not to create a hard and negative fate, because all thought is materialized. One who thinks he is persecuted by bad luck for example, places himself in a state of negativity which breeds misfortune and misery. One who possesses little self-esteem, transfers these thoughts to others who in turn will think little of him.

One of the most harmful mental habits is that of lying back in an armchair to daydream, letting one's thoughts wander freely. This habit is equivalent to opening the door of the mind to an ocean of mental vibrations from where states of depression or rage can enter. In the etheric field surrounding the earth, just like radio waves, the thoughts of all the inhabitants of the planet vibrate. Man can never be sure whether what he is thinking comes from his own brain or if his thoughts come from the external world. It is necessary to educate the imagination to have room only for beautiful, positive and optimistic thoughts; thoughts of success, peace and prosperity. In this way we will be "on the same wavelength" of everything good and positive, closing our minds to malevolent influences.

The individual who is capable of maintaining a fixed mental picture in his imagination without allowing it to be erased by other thoughts, will achieve marvels, *as mind is matter, and matter is mind*; that is, energy and matter are different manifestations of Mind.

In the energetic field, the mind is like an ovoid

which surrounds the head, an ovoid whose size is directly related to the conceptual field of the individual. This ovoid is like a closed field of electromagnetic energy which, upon intense thought, opens itself in a set direction.

All illness and mental disturbances originate when this ovoid is invaded by malignant or negative forces outside the individual, these being veritable demons caused by vice, malevolent desires, evil thoughts and wrong deeds.

In order to clarify this, we must briefly examine what happens after death. When the spirit leaves the lifeless body, a separation also takes place between the body and the animal origins of man which are an assembly of the inferior passions and evil deeds. We call this the "astral shell," since it is like a bark which covers the astral body. Normally this "shell" disintegrates after a certain time due to a lack of energy. Nevertheless when this "shell" is very strong, it fights for survival and seeks individuals in whom to introduce itself in order to continue its existence on the material plane. When one of these entities manages to enter the mental ovoid of an individual, it produces a marked character change as the individual takes on the inferior and instinctive personality traits of the deceased to whom the "shell" belonged.

All types of obsessions are a result of this phenomenon and should the shell be sufficiently powerful, it may completely dislodge the spirit of the affected individual, thus producing madness. In other more serious cases, there are various usurping entities which fight for the body, thus producing raving madness. A high percentage of insanity is due to this cause.

In some cases it is possible to expel these entities since they are afraid of pure, self-controlled individuals with strong wills and magnetic or solar characters.

Spiritualist seances are the places where these shells come to feed upon the energy of the mediums and of those who form the invocation chains. It is because of this that mediums suffer nervous exhaustion and consumption as they are surrendering their energies to these invisible vampires who mock them, pretending to be disincarnate spirits. Those most deceived and injured are the ones who attend these seances sincerely believing that the spirits of the dead will materialize. By keeping these entities alive, all those present do great harm without realizing it, because the entities absorb part of the consciousness of the participants and thus remain capable of acting consciously in their evil doings.

When science proves the existence of these beings it will be a great step toward the treatment of madness, obsessions, and mental and nervous ailments.

All illnesses originate in the mind and only after a certain period of time, do they succeed in manifesting themselves in the body.

CHAPTER V

DESIRES

The desires of the human being are numerous and varied. To desire something is as habitual and natural as breathing. Desire is another of the paths along which man squanders his mental energy. If we observe ourselves attentively, we will see that during the day we desire many things of little importance. If we abstained from these futile desires and concentrated our energy on one thing, it would be much easier to obtain what we desire, because desire is a powerful force of attraction that acts like a magnet drawing towards us that which we desire.

Desire is one of the forces which shackles the human being to matter because he is a slave to his own desires. In order to slough off these bonds, he must teach himself to develop only uplifting thoughts which are those that originate from the spirit. Far from enslaving, these thoughts liberate and uplift man.

There are also unsatisfied, instinctive and psychic desires which turn into obsessions and lead to madness.

Like thought, desire is a creative force which gives life in the energetic field to an individual whose vibrations are in harmony with the moral quality of that desire.

These invisible offspring feed on their creators and do not abandon them until they themselves materialize or die away. Purely passionate and instinctive desires are veritable bloodsuckers which penetrate the psyche and undermine its vitality.

Vice is an uncontrolled and excessive desire, that is, a formation of electro-magnetic energy which has acquired consciousness. This "desire-being" only lives if it receives on a regular basis, a certain quantity of energy which only comes from the satisfaction of the desire. As a result, it is extremely difficult to overcome a particularly strong vice, because to accomplish this, will power must be used to disintegrate the negative coagulation. Vice is easily transmitted, because in many cases, when a "desire-being" cannot drag its subject towards the vice, it seeks a more propitious field in another person. A teetotaler can be converted overnight into an habitual drinker. Incubi and succubi are solely "desire-beings" of powerful vitality; vampires which constantly seek victims upon which to feed.

There are certain individuals who deserve pity, because they are repositories of a variety of "desire-beings," each one fighting for its life and endeavoring to devour its fellows. These individuals live dominated by strong and contradictory tendencies which they are obliged to follow for the sake of peace as these vampires only give them a certain breathing space after having received their food.

It is not possible to establish how far the mental function is crippled by the actions of these creatures, but it is possible to state that a high percentage of the decisions and tendencies of an individual are dictated by these thieves who perturb one's thoughts with their passionate vibrations. An interesting example of this is the vice of cigarette smoking which brings to life a special being formed by the energy of the burning tobacco and the smoker's pleasure. This entity provokes a constant restlessness in the smoker which can only be appeased by lighting a cigarette. Based on this example, readers can analyze other "desire-beings" of more subtle natures, which keep their creators enslaved.

CHAPTER VI

SEX

Sex is life. In it is found the mystery of man's life. It may be considered as the guardian of the vital flame of all the body. When it is exhausted, death occurs.

Exoterically speaking, sex is considered only as the center of the body destined for the purpose of reproduction and is what therefore produces the differentiation between male and female. Esoterically, however, it may be considered as a powerful generating center and producer of electro-magnetic energy which continuously vibrates like electricity. This power emanates directly from the original source, that is from God, and its mission is the maintenance of life. It is due to this that life emanates from sex and from there, it is transmitted to the different centers of the body.

Nothing less than the mystery of God is hidden

in sex because its function is to create and bring to life new human beings who carry within them the divine spark. If God is our Father, it necessarily follows that He manifests Himself through sex.

As a result of religious education there actually exists a pejorative concept of sex which is symbolized many times as something obscene and injurious to man. This has been the cause of innumerable aberrations of the libido. It is necessary that sex be seen again in its true role, as the maintainer of life and that it should be definitively separated from "original sin."

Sexual education is extremely important as it is essential that human beings be taught to use sex consciously to create better lives. Men, as well as women, suffer the consequences of their scant sexual education in marriage, where they are surrounded by erroneous and antiquated concepts that prevent them in many instances from attaining true sexual harmony.

This lack of education is found especially in the younger generation who, due to a lack of adequate psychological guides, suffer from various deviations of the libido. Many turn to solitary vices while others believe that the most important proof of manhood is engaging in uncontrolled sexual activity. Parents are mostly to blame, for they generally find it "taboo" to speak of sex in front of their children. This obliges children to make their own investigations and in the majority of cases they acquire a variety of complexes and inhibitions.

It is curious to note the lack of importance given to sex, considering the fact that it is the hidden motive of a great part of human actions, as was well understood by Freud.

According to the Hermetic Principle of Generation, life is an eternal and continuous generation. Nothing can exist that has not been created by two forces, one passive or feminine and the other, active or masculine. In man is manifested the active or positive force of creative power and due to this, he does not have control over his instincts which at certain times, place him on the level of an animal which procreates impelled by magnetic currents.

Sex is the great producer, regulator and director of life, but it is also the great hypnotizer that keeps the human species in the mechanical state we have discussed in previous pages.

The Bible says that the serpent tempted Adam and Eve to eat the forbidden fruit and that their giving into that temptation was the cause for their expulsion from Paradise. In this context, Paradise symbolizes that state wherein man is in permanent contact with his own spirit. The expulsion from Paradise represents the loss of this contact when men surrendered to uncontrolled passion. By surrendering to his passions and by using sex indiscriminately, he little by little lost his faculty for perceiving reality because his sensorial impressions were so numerous and continuous as to perturb his mental function.

The Biblical symbol of the serpent as the cause of the expulsion from Paradise is curious. In it is hidden a secret to the sad mechanical condition of man. The importance given to Kundalini, or the "sleeping" serpent, is well known to lovers of Hindu literature and Yoga. It is said that this is the energy which is latent in the base of the spinal column and when it is possible to activate this energy, it opens up all kinds of magical powers. It is overlooked nevertheless that this is precisely the power which acts within the human being to keep him hypnotized and to prevent him from seeing the truth.

When man started to evolve as such on earth, he was directed by a collective spirit which guided the propagation of the species, driving couples to come together only during certain times of the year. When man acquired the power to procreate voluntarily at any moment, he freed himself from the collective spirit and began to acquire a certain degree of independence and free will.

When the objective of the sexual act is to beget a child, it is an act of creation, and each time a birth takes place, a force is produced, either good or evil, according to the quality of the union, that is to say, if it had been purely bestial or spiritual.

When there is only a union of bodies and not of

the souls, which is most common, it is the same as mechanically stimulating the sexual centers, producing perpetual dissatisfaction. Only with the simultaneous union of body and soul, is there a real deep and intimate spiritual and divine pleasure in the true sexual union. This is the difference between sinning and not sinning as far as this problem is concerned. The ones who sin are the ones who join themselves like animals.

It is not sufficient for a marriage to be legalized by the church to have the grace of God, as in Nature there are no human laws. From the viewpoint of Nature, which is perfect, a marriage consists of any couple who have formed a *matrimonial aura*, which is the union of their etheric bodies on the invisible plane. When this matrimonial aura is absent, a marriage can still be legalized and blessed by the church, but it will be false and a lie as there will only have been a coupling of bodies. For the neophytes, I will explain that the etheric double is a body of subtle matter which is invisible and which is indissolubly bound to the physical body, being its exact replica. All alterations of the double are immediately manifested in the physical body.

Everything sexual revolves around one thing: etheric magnetism. In all sexual contact between man and woman there is a great interchange of magnetism. These magnetic vibrations strongly influence the happiness or misfortune of the individual. A person with bad luck or with a pessimistic, unfortunate and unhappy magnetic vibration will transmit this at the time of union.

Magnetism is what produces sexual attraction and the experience of "falling in love," and it is represented by the symbol of Eros or Cupid. Due to this, many infatuations terminate abruptly, having produced a magnetic discharge, because the love in its vulgar manifestation was only a drunkenness or saturation of etheric magnetism.

In the field of amorous attraction, the more magnetism a woman possesses, the more she will attract the opposite sex, even if she has little physical appeal. What has been called "sex-appeal" is the attractive power of magnetism which is invisible and intangible. It is common to see many beautiful women without this power of attraction for men because they lack sexual, etheric magnetism.

There are people who inherently lead healthy lives, and possessing great self-control, are great accumulators of magnetism and veritable natural magnets with attractive powers, both economical and sentimental.

There are women, on the other hand, who are always unlucky in love in spite of being physically attractive because they lack the power of magnetic attraction. If they marry, they are not capable of holding the man for long and are in the end, abandoned.

I will offer here some instructions so that both men and women may accumulate an abundance of electro-magnetic energy, which will help them to triumph in life.

Sexual magnetic power is lost through three main channels which we must finally eliminate in order to produce a gradual accumulation. These channels are: negative emotions, uncontrolled desires, and negative imaginative states.

There is a close relationship between emotional and instinctive states. A woman, during a jealous crisis, for example, expends her magnetism uselessly, losing her attractiveness to men and ages prematurely because life flows from her. A jealous, irritable and domineering woman expels her sexual energy through her heart and gradually becomes unattractive.

For a woman to be very attractive to men, she must first of all have great control over her feelings, so that her heart will not disperse the magnetism produced and accumulated by sex. When she attains this dominion over her psyche, she must achieve mastery over her instinctive self and imaginative self. By achieving this, everything will be within her reach. Man, on the other hand, should give preferential attention to educating and dominating his sexual side, which is his weak point or Achilles heel.

Within the education of the desires, we find a great source of energy. If a person can deny himself the satisfaction of a passing desire and keep this current of energy alive, he will be able to augment the volume of his magnetic energy. For example, an individual receives some very good news and his first impulse is to run and tell his friends and family. If he consciously postpones this desire for a few days, he will accumulate a certain quantity of magnetism.

With regards to the imagination, it is necessary to attain a certain state of control which will eliminate negative and morbid thoughts and will allow only optimistic and cheerful ones.

A man who wishes to attract a woman must be sincere, gallant, understanding, strong but sensitive, masculine and virile. He must have an alert and powerful mind, since if in women beauty is both physical and within the soul, in man it is in his intelligence. The more intelligent the man, the more beautiful he appears in the eyes of a woman.

Women more than anything else, seek support from a man in every way and he must therefore be ready to supply the strength she lacks. Man and woman embody the two great principles of Strength and Beauty.

A woman who wants to attract and keep a man must develop the following characteristics: profound femininity, sweetness, comprehension and beauty of the soul. She must be wife, lover, friend, sister and mother. She must never make the man feel enslaved or deprived of his liberty.

The key to a couple's happiness resides in mutual tolerance and in being more willing to give than to receive.

Nevertheless, in order to have perfect sexual harmony in a couple, it is necessary to erase all the instinctive and the psychic wounds received during the course of their lives. These are what cause the majority of failures in marriage. It is not unusual, for example, for a man who has been very pampered by his mother during childhood, to seek a woman who will assume the same role and from whom he will demand the same attention a mother gives a child. It is also common for a woman to seek a father substitute. All this greatly influences the first sexual experience and sets the course for future life. A man whose first sexual experience was with a prostitute for example, will seek to marry a woman similar to a vendor of love.

If the first sexual union in man is important, in woman it is what decisively determines the course of her future life, her happiness or unhappiness, for a woman who is a virgin, resembles a blank page waiting to be written upon.

It is quite a common occurrence for a woman to arrive to her wedding night with many illusions only to be taken brutally by an instinctive and passionate man, which thus creates in her a profound subconscious aversion to men. If she later seeks happiness with another, the ghost of her first experience will always haunt her and could be the cause of complete frigidity.

Another deviation of the libido, which occurs frequently in women, is auto-eroticism, that is, when she seeks to excite herself by erotic images of jealousy in order to increase the pleasure of the sexual act. This also applies to the one who starts a quarrel just to surrender to the man at the height of the quarrel and then abruptly from there, pass into amorous delight.

All these refinements or sexual complexes should be erased from the subconscious by means of adequate mental hygiene and rigid self-discipline. When will power is not sufficient to accomplish this, the individual should place himself under the guidance of a person who is able to erase these impressions from the cerebral neurons, and in difficult cases, this can only be done by a psychiatrist with profound knowledge of the great mystery of the mind.

The erotic imaginations of a woman can so completely influence her companion that he may well deceive her if she imagines so, because the imaginative vibrations she sends oblige him to actualize them.

Once all these negative recordings have disappeared, a natural, healthy union of equilibrium can be produced, which is the only kind that leads to harmony and happiness.

Another case that must be mentioned, due to its importance, is that of the masculine woman. Masculinity is produced in a woman when she is united with a man who is weak in character and she is strong and dominating. Little by little, she becomes more active and masculine and the man more timid and depressed as she is absorbing all his masculine magnetism, leaving him only with a passive or feminine magnetism. The masculine magnetism which this woman absorbs, develops in her marked masculine characteristics: strength, power, domination, aggressiveness, impulsiveness, bossiness, audacity and decisiveness, and the man becomes ever more feminine until he is incapable of making decisions, handing over the reins totally to the woman. If this couple has sons, they too will be victims of this whirlwind of absorption which has transformed this woman and they will fall entirely under her influence and show marked feminine characteristics as their masculine magnetism has been absorbed by their mother. This absorption can lead these children to sexual inversion.

Neither men nor women are aware that they exhibit in their characters, certain traits of the opposite sex. A man, for example, could show the following characteristics which are normally identified with women, such as jealousy, indecisiveness, fear, volubility, passiveness and hysteria; while the woman, anxious to dominate the man, desires to transform and possess him. All this obscures the great secret of magnetism which is, that men as well as women, carry a certain percentage of the traits of the opposite sex.

True and sincere students will understand this mystery in all its magnitude.

The correct use of sex is the basis of occult spiritual development. It is a cause for sadness to see all those occultist beginners who believe that it is sufficient to sing mantras, practice yoga breathing or chant prayers to the highest to attain illumination. It is equally sad to see those who seek development through certain Hindu traditions which call for celibacy in men as a means to attain magical powers, because, in the end, many of them become feminized or inverted due to becoming magnetically depolarized.

In connection with the subject of sex, it is necessary to denounce the crime committed against the fetus during the mother's pregnancy if she continues sexual relations after becoming pregnant. The being which is within the mother, receives at the moment of sexual union, a strong current of sexual energy which remains profoundly engraved on its fragile nature, provoking after its birth a premature sexual awakening and a variety of unbalanced emotional conditions, as well as sexual inversion. During this delicate period the woman should abstain from all strong emotions, quarrels and worries, and should shun any depressive atmosphere.

It is lamentable that man has not studied more deeply the means of improving the human species, but instead dedicates his time to perfecting certain breeds of animals.

To conclude this chapter we present the key to sexual magnetism:

Man is active, the one who gives, the one who seeks and must necessarily give continuously. Woman is passive, constantly seeking to be absorbed or to take everything within her in order to conceive. He is the creator and she the coagulator. These two forces give origin to a third force, which is the child.

From this union is born the Binary, and subsequently, the Ternary.

To reach perfection, the Binary should be converted into unity.

By studying active and passive magnetism, it is possible to comprehend the true sense of the union between man and woman.

CHAPTER VII

GOD

God is All. Everything that exists and everything that does not exist is within God. Nothing can exist outside of Him.

From the hermetic point of view we will call God *"the great universal mind,"* that is, the essence from which everything has emerged and to which everything will return: the vital spark which is found in all minerals, in vegetables and in man. Everything that exists in the Universe, be it matter or energy, is formed in essence by mind, the sole, infinite and eternal energy manifested in the infinitely small or the infinitely large. Because everything that exists has emerged from All, the All is similar to the womb which has in itself the shape of all things. The All is the substantial Reality which is hidden behind all manifestations of life. *It is the great father-mother which created itself, which has always existed and which will exist forever.*

God created life so as to grow in consciousness and intelligence, capturing through man's multiple experiences the most perfect manifestation of this universal essence.

Throughout the entire Universe, we are aware that everything continually flows and ebbs, everything changes and evolves, everything is born and everything dies, but the substantial energy or mind grows constantly and expands toward the infinite, its essence remaining unaltered.

God is infinite, eternal, absolute and immutable and therefore, everything finite, alterable and transitory cannot be the All; and as in reality nothing exists outside the All, that which is finite or transformable "is nothing," or in other words, is illusory.

Understanding this, Occultism maintains that "all is illusion," certainly in relation to the absolute, because as far as man is concerned, what is real to him is everything that he perceives through his senses.

Similarly, with relation to man's consciousness, *all is illusion.* From the view point of the absolute for example, time does not exist, but we are aware that for man, time is a reality.

The Universe is composed of *relative realities* and *absolute realities.*

This explains why everything is matter, and at the same time, everything is energy. Matter is nothing but energy in a denser vibratory state. Matter and energy represent the two poles of the manifestation of the mind. Matter is the denser vibration, and spirit is the more subtle.

All the Universe is a mental creation and we can therefore affirm that *we exist within the mind of God.*

From the moment we recognize that God is Mind and that the mind manifests itself in man, we can comprehend the possibility of being able to join that great intelligence.

This is the study of Occultism; *the education of the individual so he may manifest in all its power, the divine spark within himself, that is, the part of the great universal mind which lives within him.*

The conception of God is so vague and absurd for most people that it must be difficult for them to comprehend God as we have presented Him, which is the only concept that reason, logic and science permits.

Atheists, who do not believe in God deserve compassion as they deny their own existence, denying the air, sun and life itself.

The most widespread concept of God is that of an old man with a white beard who is in heaven, the heaven where all those who have not sinned go and where they eternally praise Him.

This idea is all very well for those lazy ones who do not wish to bother with thinking about God or themselves, and who prefer to accept the various dogmas that religions prescribe. The one who desires to know God more fully, must be dedicated to study all His manifestations in order to comprehend His essence. As man is the most perfect manifestation of the Great Universal Mind, it is necessary that he make a conscious study of himself in order to know God at least in the level that his conceptual state will permit.

The key to the study and knowledge of God is contained within the Hermetic aphorism: *"All is mind, the universe is mental."*

If we can clearly understand that "all is mind," we will have forged ahead in the investigation of the mysteries of life. This energy that we call God, is manifested in the form of a double force, creative on one hand and destructive on the other. Both are mutually in balance. The creative force is permanently creating and giving life, that is, generating. The destructive force seeks at all times to destroy in order to create a more perfect form of life. That which the layman calls the devil, is nothing more than the counterpart or shadow of God. If we apply the Hermetic aphorism which says, "as it is below, so it is above and as it is above, so it is below," we will be able to see that the entire Universe, with its planets, galaxies, suns and gods may be found in an identical form within man, and thus even more so both the creative and destructive forces.

When he prays, man places himself in contact with the energy of God that is within him and therefore it is absurd to pretend to find God in the external, when He is found within man. Everything positive emanates from God's creative energy. Love, happiness, optimism, serenity and the desire to help others are manifestations of the divine generating force. Depression, pessimism, morbid thoughts, hate, jealousy and possessive love are manifestations of the destructive or disintegrating force. Therefore it is important only to be in contact with the generating part of God, in order to avoid the actions of the disintegrating force which cause old age and decrepitude. Melancholia and sadness, for example, are powerfully destructive forces which little by little sap the reserve of positive energy of the organism until illness and death result. Happiness, on the other hand, is a powerful, positive force which we should constantly endeavor to be in touch with in every moment. We should rejoice in the simple things of Nature, enjoying the fresh morning air, the song of the birds and the flowering of the trees.

Nature is the manifestation of the feminine part of God in the earth. She is abundance, the creative force and the vigorous power of vital life. All the great secrets of life lie within Nature, for she is like an open book for those who are able to read and for those who know how to penetrate into the secrets of her multiple manifestations. Nature is our loving mother who at all times watches over the welfare of her children; but when man breaks her laws, he sets himself against her and loses her protection. Among the laity, there are the mistaken beliefs fostered by certain religions that God punishes us when we sin, and these religions go further by casting into hell those who do not follow their dogmas or precepts. God, as the spiritual force of *all life* and *all love* is constantly inspiring us, just as the sun shines on the sinner, the saint or the criminal, His light reaching everyone equally. Could it be possible that God is a vengeful and fickle entity whose favor can be won over by prayers? God, as the infinite source of life and love, always seeks our spiritual development and our welfare, but as creator and keeper of life, He has produced a set of laws which are indispensable for the maintenance of life. When man breaks these laws he destroys the harmony of life within himself and encounters pain and misery, that is, he punishes himself when he sets himself up against Nature. It is curious how God is always forgotten and how we run to and request from Him only selfish material possessions or the achievement of all passionate desires. In the case of war or any major catastrophe, either personal or collective, we immediately cry to God, but as soon as the catastrophe is over, we again forget Him and surrender ourselves to material pleasures.

Without a doubt, instinctively the most profound desire and yearning of each human being is to unite with God — in other words, to find God within himself. Some seek this through mysticism and the domination of their desires, and others choose the terrible path of sensual and material rapture. From the criminal to the saint, from the sage to the beggar, all human beings instinctively seek to find themselves and strive toward a union with the divine.

The only wise way to find God is through the practice of the highest spiritual virtues, practicing love towards all human beings without distinction of class or color, serving and helping others according to one's own strengths, by being tolerant, respectful, good citizens, good friends, good fathers and good sons. It means to practice all virtues that are within the reach of man as a representative of God upon earth, but to practice them from the heart without becoming bleached sepulchers who cover themselves with great virtues, while their souls are mean and corrupt.

He who desires to find God should remember that the greatest wisdom is to "love one and all," and to remember that one who has achieved more should be more humble and ready to help and nurture others. He should never forget that pride, vanity and arrogance are the greatest enemies of the human being.

God is only reached through the doorway labeled: *love and service.*

CHAPTER VIII

THE MYSTERIES
OF LIFE AND DEATH

In order to be successful in life and to wisely practice the "art of living," it is necessary to have a basic knowledge of life and death, and to similarly understand what destiny is.

If we accept that man has a spirit and a body, we will be able to logically understand that if the body ages and dies, the spirit, on the other hand perpetually remains young and is immortal.

Can God who is unfolded within our spirit, die? This eternal question immediately arises when we consider the matter of body and spirit. Why must we live in a material body, when we could live eternally in the spiritual state?

The reason for the incarnation of the spirit in a body must be sought in God. As spirits, we are part of God and must cooperate with His great work of perfection and expansion of Himself. On the one hand, we make ourselves perfect through the multiple experiences we face in our lives and on the other hand, we represent God on earth bringing about the evolution of matter. The great human work is to give consciousness to matter, or better said, to "spiritualize" matter.

Man must undergo many experiences before he attains spiritual perfection and before he acquires sufficient consciousness to comprehend God, his spirit must dwell within many bodies to acquire different experiences; this is what is known as reincarnation.

In this succession of lives, Nature works with wisdom and kindness by erasing from our minds all memories, which remain engraved only in the form of experiences or in the potential abilities of the individual.

It is necessary to clarify that reincarnation is not possible for everyone, as there are many who do not reincarnate, because there exists nothing that survives the physical death of their bodies. Upon death, they disintegrate and are reabsorbed by their original source or the Great Universal Soul.

HOW ONE IS BORN
In the space surrounding the earth are found the spirits of all those who have already gone through the process of purification after death and all those who are ready to be reborn into material life.

These spirits vibrate at different heights, which are directly related to the level of consciousness they have attained. Those who are inferior remain a few yards above the earth, and those who have reached the conceptual development of an Einstein, for example, are beyond the stratosphere. When a couple are joined in the creative act, a veritable streak of electro-magnetic light is launched into space and this light, in its magnitude, is in direct relation to the moral, emotional and spiritual quality of both. If this lightning reaches, for example, 1500 feet in height, it will choose from the "I's" which are there and which are most harmonious with the vibrations of the parents. This electro-magnetic force attracts an Ego like a giant magnet and it penetrates through the head of the father, until it reaches the sperm and enters the mother. When it passes through the father, it shares his spiritual-mental vibration and during the nine months of pregnancy it receives the vibrations of the mother.

This period of gestation is the most important to the destiny of the unborn being, as it receives a constant discharge of diverse vibrations from the mother which strongly influence its future life on earth.

LIFE AND FATE

The newborn begins his terrestrial life the moment he breathes his first breath, and at that moment, the vibrations of the cosmic rays that constantly bombard the earth, begin to be recorded within him. The combination of cosmic rays, which are ruled by the different planetary positions, form what we call Destiny.

Fate is formed by four principle causes: **1)** the karma brought from other lives, that is, the assembly of good or bad deeds which have taken place in other lives and whose effects must be expiated in the present one; **2)** that which is received from the parents; **3)** that which is received from the position of the planets at the moment of birth, and **4)** the sum total of all experiences undergone up until the age of 33, which is the age when one begins to live out the causes created in youth.

During all his life, man is just a slave to his fate and lives entirely unconscious of this slavery.

The oriental proverb, "everything is written," contains great wisdom as the occult judges or "Lords of Destiny" are the divine powers who direct human destiny, determining before the individual is born what his life will be on earth, in other words, his Fate.

The Hermeticist is able to predict the future of a person by observing his map of destiny, which has been traced before incarnation.

The beggar, as well as the king, has been

assigned a destiny which has been traced according to experiences that are necessary for his development.

When the Hermeticist attains an elevated state of consciousness, he becomes the master of his own destiny, because he conquers the forces which endeavor to impel him towards experiences he no longer needs since he has become conscious.

This is the most notable difference between the Initiate and the man who is unaware of Nature's laws. The Initiate lives fully conscious, knowing perfectly well where he is going, while the other lives like a leaf in the wind.

DEATH

Once a man has come to the end of the terrestrial cycle which was assigned to him in his present physical body, the transformation we call death comes, which is only the birth into another life.

At the moment of the separation between the spirit and the body, one is born into the field of energy, which is a life totally distinct from the physical, as it is not possible to enjoy the material pleasures to which one was once accustomed.

Because the law is that children feed from their parents, the newly disincarnated must face all the mental forms born from their passions, desires and feelings encountered during their lives on earth. From this is born the belief in hell, for it is a veritable hell for those who have surrendered to base human passions, because their spiritual children face them in the form of horrible demons that endeavor to continue feeding off of them. In order to evolve, they must overcome all their evil inclinations and weaknesses until the disintegration of the children born of their passions is attained. Once this is accomplished, there is a period of rest on the higher levels until they are fit to return to life again.

One who has lived a pure and noble life on earth will, upon death, be surrounded by angels who are his own spiritual children and who will help him to rise to the invisible planes.

For one who has not taken the trouble to cultivate himself spiritually and morally, death is a constant threat and appears as something horrible in his eyes. This is not the case for one who has reached a higher state of consciousness, because death for him is a new life, and he is absolutely unafraid, since he is certain of having acted always according to the dictates of his conscience.

Nonbelievers and materialists doubt that there exists a life after death and maintain that after death all is finished. These "thinkers" do not take the trouble to reason in accordance with science which maintains that nothing is lost in the Universe and that everything is transformed.

Nothing dies; everything passes to another state of existence.

Can a word die after having been uttered? Can a thought die?

CHAPTER IX

ANGUISH

AND HUMAN PROBLEMS

Knowledge that cannot be put into practice is useless. In this book, the aim is to place the teachings of Occultism into their correct perspective; a perspective that is within the grasp of all and that requires no previous study in order to make use of the instructions given herein.

It is my wish to avoid all the complicated terms that are commonly used in treatises on Occultism, because they require one to be learned in that discipline in order to be able to decipher them. In many of these books, the truth has deliberately been hidden, because it is sometimes dangerous to shout these truths openly.

In ancient times, occult knowledge was only taught to a chosen few who had undergone terrible tests of a physical, moral and spiritual character; but in this era of materialism and confusion, it is necessary to reveal this science as far as secrecy permits, in order to inspire and help those who desire to pursue higher studies or for those who simply wish to improve themselves in any way, whether it be economically, emotionally or psychologically.

There are some people who have serious problems and who, although they look for help to solve them, do not know where to find it, lifting their eyes in vain to heaven. If Occultism is mentioned, they smile incredulously in the same way that science does. To them I would suggest that they first practice the advice given in this book and only afterwards judge the results.

If a thousand years ago someone said that man would be able to talk across a wire, that there would be a box where living images would appear and that men would travel in vehicles which could move by themselves, people would have laughed and called the author of such statements crazy.

With time, all the marvelous powers of Occultism like telepathy, clairvoyance and other lesser known ones, will be matters of public domain, practiced on a daily basis. Everything is a question of evolution. More or less time will elapse for the acquiring of consciousness and intelligence. If we just thought about the relativity of time, we would be able to comprehend that there exists a science which can enormously accelerate the development of human consciousness to unknown limits.

This science has been kept and continues to be

kept secret, because humanity is not prepared to receive it, not having attained a sufficient degree of moral and spiritual perfection.

The one who constantly practices goodness, fraternal love and human virtues elevates himself spiritually, thus deserving to receive this knowledge which is impossible to acquire without preparation.

Due to a mistaken attitude produced by the tremendous materialism of our age, everyone seeks happiness through material possessions; the obtaining of wealth and fortune being the most important, because with these, people expect to have achieved everything in life. But after much complication and confusion, people are left with disgust and deception, because there are so few who arrive at true happiness, something which should be the birthright and legitimate right of human beings on earth.

What can one achieve by having great riches if one is weakened with spiritual hunger and thirst?

Youth, with its eternal disregard for the future, lives thinking only of today. Only when one reaches old age and realizes that time has gone by too rapidly and that much of what one really yearned for has not been attained, does one bitterly ask; "What have I done in my life? What will I leave behind on earth after I die?"

Unfortunately (or fortunately), no one is born with knowledge and it is necessary to live 50 or 60 years before reaching the age of discernment required for avoiding mistakes. Paradoxically, when this wisdom and knowledge of the art of living is finally acquired, the body starts to decay due to old age, and death happens just when an adequate state of consciousness to attain true happiness has been reached. This apparent injustice gives us much to think about. We should meditate on the question: "What mysterious power gives us life without our consent and then, once we have learned how to enjoy it, takes it away?"

Naturally, not everyone takes advantage of experience and many people reach old age as ignorant as, or more so, than in youth.

There are many universities, schools and centers of study which cater to the civilized world, making one proud of the degree of culture attained, but nowhere are there schools which teach the most necessary and difficult of all sciences: *the art of living*.

The final result of a life is merely a question of accident or chance, produced by the great law which governs the animal kingdom: *the survival of the fittest.*

It is truly miraculous that young and healthy people, with normal intellectual and spiritual concerns, can still become professionals, because they encounter so much mystery, spiritual abandonment, hate, egoism, ignorance and so many unknown and unsolvable circumstances. It is strange that their minds do not become unhinged with the numerous and tremendous contradictions. Success is generally for those who cover their eyes and ears so as not to see or hear anything, remaining insensitive to the multitude of human problems.

Many who have been able to glimpse the truth, suddenly end with mental perturbances or insanity.

Parents transmit to their children their personal concept of life, which is related to their own experiences and knowledge and not to the immutable and eternal laws of Nature. For this reason, children find their parents "old fashioned" and feel misunderstood by them.

Both psychology and psychiatry make the effort to condition the psyche so that life can be faced under better conditions, but they are unable to deal with certain psychic manifestations which are beyond orthodox knowledge.

If psychologists were initiated into the mysteries of the mind as part of their education, they could contribute to changing the psychic state in their patients, eliminating all that is bad and negative.

All young people have serious emotional and spiritual problems which generally are not understood by their parents and because of these problems, they make mistakes which could have been avoided if they had been "in their right mind." I say "in their right mind" because, when problems of any kind turn into dangerous obsessions, the mental and emotional stability of the individual weakens and he can no longer be responsible for his actions as he loses his power to reason.

Religious consolation does not satisfy modern man who is always wishing to know the "why" and the scientific cause of all things.

I do not wish in any way to injure the sensibilities of those with religious faith, but only wish to show that as there are individuals who are content to accept the religious dogmas of a faith, there are also others who seek answers by way of reason, knowledge and by learning the causes.

For those who seek the path of knowledge, Occultism signals the attainment of that path, because it is marked by serene, intelligent and unbiased investigation through which it is possible to understand the hidden causes of all the phenomena which we perceive through our senses and our mind.

The art of living is so simple and so difficult at the same time and the secret to it all is found in the saying *"love one another."*

Unfortunately, the human being is weak and lacks will power, stability, unity and consciousness. He is so weak that he is perpetually accosted by a multitude of desires, ambitions, hate, egotism, vanity and various passions which block the way to higher achievement.

All of these passional states form a real prison for the spirit as it becomes incapable of fully enjoying life in the body, and of expressing itself, its thoughts, desires and capabilities through this vehicle. The spirit, which is perfect in essence because it is an emanation of God, is dragged down by the savage, animal-like and passionate material plane, where the actions committed go against the spirit's desire for greater evolution.

Rather than the body serving the spirit, the spirit has been obliged to serve the body, having been totally displaced and erased by the selfish desires of the body, which seeks those satisfactions pertinent to its own condition.

It is for this reason that the abuse of purely physical satisfactions such as drinking, eating and various sensual refinements, produces a tremendous internal dissatisfaction, which is the reaction of the spirit being forced to commit acts against its higher condition.

One habit which brings severe consequences is the habit of satisfying all bodily desires as soon as they arise. One may imagine that ultimate happiness is the power to enjoy all kinds of material comforts, even though one lives in a poverty stricken spiritual state. The intelligent, fraternal and spiritually sensitive man is frequently looked upon as someone of little value, if he does not have a large bank account or a luxurious car. Those who have great wealth are received with respect everywhere, all the world pays them homage and all doors are open to them. They form a kind of millionaire's aristocracy and look down on those who are not wealthy. By contrast, it is curious what can be observed on the spiritual level or plane of energy, which is commonly called the fourth dimension. There, spiritual aristocracy exists; a brotherhood accessible only to those who have been able to transform the base metal of their souls into spiritual gold, that is, for those who have overcome all weaknesses and passions, replacing them with virtues. On the plane of energy therefore, an important business man, elegantly dressed and driving a luxurious car, can look like a beggar, bearing horrible demons on his shoulders. Those demons are the material possessions which have made him a slave to his wealth. He does not own his house; the house owns him. He does not own his car; the car owns him. Yet a humble caretaker on this same plane of energy, can be a great gentleman, dressed in snowy-white, beautiful clothes.

Life is a gigantic stage with millions of actors each wearing the mask appropriate to the part assigned to him by the stage director, or God.

The difference between the theater and reality is that in reality, each individual plays many parts and has many masks and disguises, one for each occasion. He is obliged to assume different roles to impress others and to reaffirm his personality. After he plays these parts for some time, he confuses them so much with reality, that they come to form part of his psyche.

These masks help keep the individual in the depths of ignorance with regards to reality because he perceives everything according to the part he plays.

The trite recommendation, "know thyself," is converted into an impossibility amidst the profusion of masks.

Imagine a play in which each actor wishes to interpret his own role without taking the other actors or stage director into account and you will have a rather good idea of what happens with the human soul. The stage is so confused with reality that man is incapable of objectively perceiving what he receives through his senses. All man's perception is subjective, and he therefore lives in ignorance, consumed by pain, illness and the fear of death, in spite of having all the wisdom of the Universe within him.

This distortion in the thinking principle of the individual is the real Tower of Babel which initiated the total and complete incomprehension of the human race. All human deeds are conditioned by external events which influence in one way or the other the state of an individual, to sway towards certain decisions.

There are a few authentic manifestations of the "I" or spirit which can be considered as being on the plane of consciousness.

Most manifestations are produced by diverse

pressures exerted on the psyche by something that penetrates the senses, or by vibratory states which are recorded in the subconscious by all the experiences which lead up to the moments of expression.

The study of Occultism is the study of oneself for the purpose of distinguishing between what is real and unreal, between what is authentic and artificial. We could call reality *the spirit*, and what is not real, *the personality*.

From here on we shall consider the personality as that living part of man which he has obtained through inheritance, education, environment and pleasant or unpleasant experiences.

The opposite of the personality is the essence of man, which is the irradiation of the spirit.

Understanding fully what has just been said above, isn't it odd to hear someone say, "I want to do such and such a thing," or, "my opinion is as follows."

Is it possible for a machine to have an opinion or to wish to do something?

Is it possible to talk about the consciousness of a machine, the will of a machine or the love of a machine? Modern robots created by scientists are nothing new; they are simply caricatures of the human being.

These robots are programmed through their different circuits to always act in the same way under specific circumstances. The reaction is determined by the particular circuit. It is easy to understand that it is impossible for one of these robots "to think for itself," that is, to perform deeds which are not previously recorded in its circuits, being able nevertheless, to combine the information contained in them. In the moment that it performs this way, it will have acquired consciousness. Man is the same as these robots. He always thinks, feels and reacts according to the combination of his different circuits. This is not reality, nor is it objective; these are circuits recorded in his psyche by diverse circumstances.

The state into which man has fallen, is termed in Occultism, "to be asleep." The human being is in a deep sleep, because everything that happens to him is as if it were dreamt behind the thick veil of his diverse circuits. Everything physically agreeable or pleasing contributes to making this sleep deeper.

This is the reason for all the fasting, privations, torments and discipline of mystics who seek the development of their consciousness. These disciplines make the body "uncomfortable," shaking it into wakening from its lethargy. The worst aspect of this peculiar state of sleep is that no one is aware of it, and when someone is told about it, he laughs ironically and says, "How can I be asleep? Can't you see that I am awake?"

The inability to recognize this state of sleep immediately hinders all possibilities for progress, as it is impossible to ask someone to fight something whose existence is denied.

It is possible to recognize this state of sleep only by careful self-observation and self-analysis. How different then is the concept of pleasure and pain! All pleasure that is purely physical favors the sleep state, and all pain, whether physical or moral, shakes up and dissipates the sleep.

The one who has fully awakened has no need of pain to evolve.

Due to its importance, let us examine more carefully the matter of consciousness.

If we observe ourselves attentively, we will find that in daily life we tend to identify with and let our awareness be pulled toward everything that catches our attention. The more our attention is attracted to a certain thing, the more easily we lose the awareness of ourselves, because our attention displaces our consciousness in favor of the object to which it is attracted.

This is when identification between the individual and the stimulus is born; the identification renders him entirely asleep or unconscious.

Is it possible for an individual to be fully awake if he has no consciousness of *self*?

The "I," or spirit, lives imprisoned in a web of sensations which are constantly reaching the brain. The impressions which are felt through the senses are many. The imagination works rapidly during the day without a moment's rest. All these sensations are the obstacles which prevent us from becoming conscious. If we examine the psyche of several individuals, we will find marked differences in the development of their consciousness. On the lowest level is the person whose center of life is entirely focused in the physical body, who lets the instinctive forces predominate his thoughts and emotions. In another, the center of psychic life is in the heart, where emotion persists above everything else, and this man lives solely through his emotions. At a slightly higher level, is the intellectual, whose psychic center is in the brain. This man uses his reason in everything and considers everything mentally.

These three types of man form current humanity, machine-men or automatons.

Above these types of men is a totally unknown category of human beings, of which only flashes of their genius have been gleaned. Nobody knows how they have risen above those born from women, to be transformed into sons of God, or "twice-born."

Lineage, wealth and social status are not conditions that guarantee this transformation, because this process does not depend on material things. They are simply human beings who have attained what all humans imagine they have, and that is a will of their own, freedom, consciousness, liberty, etc.

In order to get an idea of the development of

these chosen people (many are called but few are chosen), we will establish a brief classification.

On the lowest plane, we find the man who could have been born in any of the groups described above, but who has soared above his group by having come into contact with a school of Occultism. He acquires an "I" or psychic center which is more or less stable, and he begins to know himself. He, nevertheless, still faces the possibility of falling behind and returning to the sleep state, of reverting to his original condition, because what he has attained is not yet permanent. It has not become flesh of his flesh and blood of his blood.

On a higher plane, we find the man who has attained physical crystallization, that is, one who has been able to fuse his soul into one unit and has been able to redirect it. Naturally, it is possible that this crystallization took a wrong direction, and if so, this person could not reach perfection unless he decides on an instant reversal and proceeds to unite with that which was crystallized. Once this has been done, the way is open for a new crystallization in agreement with what he desires.

At the summit of this road of perfection, is the man who has been able to attain the most complete development and evolution possible to a human being, and who has attained forever, will, consciousness, immortality, the dominion over matter, etc.

All occult development is centered in the soul of

an individual. He must first eliminate all that is negative and undesirable, replacing it with positive characteristics, and subsequently joining all the strong currents of the soul under the guidance of the "I" and the will.

If we analyze the soul and understand its extreme complexity, we will discover the hidden motives which impel us to act or react in one way or another.

Within us are forces which prevent us from functioning well; complexes, inhibitions and negative or dismotivated feelings and thoughts. Our life depends much more than we think upon our soul. All that manifests later in the physical body, originates in the soul. If a man is ill, it is because his soul is sick. If he ages, it is because his soul has aged. If "bad luck" follows him and he attains nothing in life, it is due to the condition of his soul.

It is extremely difficult to see ourselves and to recognize our own limitations and mistakes because generally the cause of our misfortunes lie deep within our psyche.

It is through the soul that the positive and negative powers to which we have previously referred, arise.

According to the predominant forces within us, we elevate or debase ourselves daily.

It is the destructive power which takes over when we are pessimistic, discouraged, sad, melancholic or timid. The man who is successful, on the other hand, has learned consciously or unconsciously, to unite himself with the constructive power using his will, feelings and imagination to that end. Later on, we will give instructions for the practical use of this powerful force.

In this chapter we will concentrate on examining man's problems, both large and small, which arise entirely from the combination of Spirit and Mass.

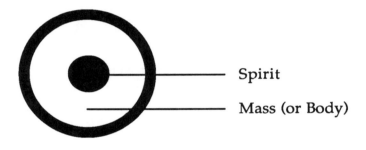

By remembering that we are spirits in animal bodies, we will understand the eternal conflict within each human being; the conflict between the "I" and the body or *mass*. Of course, it is not possible to be identified with anything other than the physical body, since this is the vehicle of the spirit. The body is the material form which covers the spirit in order for it to be able to act on the physical plane. As the spirit and body are opposite poles of the same power called Mind, life on earth is a real imprisonment for the individual who has not educated his body in order to serve his spirit. For the most part, in the human race, the spirit serves the body and becomes a true slave to it, at all times being forced to relinquish its energy to satisfy the mass. This is precisely what man fails to realize; that the spirit, which is a super-conscious and super-intelligent power, is the servant of the mass, which is unconscious and raw material.

From this arises all human misfortunes, conflicts, contradictions, illnesses and pain.

Occultism is the science of becoming conscious and intelligent, of educating the mass so that the spirit may act with full power and intelligence.

It is the real union with God, the union with one's own spirit, the union with one's self.

Any spiritual discipline which does not spring from this foundation is false and capricious. Nothing can be gained by the one who endeavors to reach God, without first having conquered and educated himself.

Many pseudo-occultists claim to have reached cosmic consciousness or union with God. It would not be difficult to prove that they have not even become conscious of themselves, which is an important step toward attaining cosmic consciousness.

We must always start by becoming conscious of the material world and to become aware of our exact position, because from the moment we begin life within the physical body, we must not forget our position as we endeavor to reach unknown heights.

The five-pointed star or the pentagram, which represents man with legs and arms outstretched, is well known in Occultism. This star is used because it represents an ideal, that of the man whose consciousness and spirit have entire dominion over his body.

The profane being who serves the world of matter, is represented by the inverted star, in which the body dominates over the spirit.

One who has realized the symbolism of the pentagram lives a very different life from the one who has not developed his spiritual skills. Physically, his existence may be similar to that of any other man, but psychically he lives in an entirely different world, a world where there is no ugliness, hate, fear, death, pain or destruction.

The occultist is a true scientist who has learned to consciously direct his vehicle or his body. This same body, to the profane man, is an extremely complicated machine which dominates and manages him.

Pentagram (Occultist)   Inverted (Worldly)

This fantastic vehicle we know as the human body, is managed by the Initiate as an enormous power plant connecting and disconnecting circuits at will. If his mind works too rapidly, the mental circuit is disconnected and he becomes inactive. If the Initiate desires a change in personality in order to understand others in another intellectual or social sphere, his vibratory state is adjusted to the environment within which he wishes to act. If his liver or stomach ails him, he establishes an electrical overcharge on those circuits, filling the sick organs with life, changing illness into health.

Naturally, this is not accomplished in a short time, and it is the reason why many students of Occultism become disheartened at not being able to acquire practical results quickly.

For the Initiate who has managed to reach total and complete dominion over matter, nothing is impossible, because he can rejuvenate his physical body and live on earth for a length of time that would seem incredible to the profane.

Let us recall the Hermetic aphorism which says: "Everything is Mind, the Universe is Mental."

This is the ultimate key for all human fulfillment.

All possibilities are contained within this aphorism. Meditating carefully on this, it is possible to understand many things. It can be understood that the cause of all our difficulties lies within ourselves and that by changing our mental state, we will triumph.

If we understand that *all is Mind*, we will see that our body is *mental energy, contained or coagulated in a specific vibration.* Our brain, our liver, and our heart are also mental matter through which we can manifest our thoughts.

With strict self-discipline, the Initiate gains control over the mental or atomic matter of his entire body and is able to prevail over the physical through his mind.

Since we are speaking about the physical body, let us analyze physical imbalance, known as illness.

Generally medical science is limited and only knows how to treat the symptoms of an illness as if it were the poisonous fruit of a tree, while the cause of that illness, like the roots of a tree, remain hidden in the soul. The tree continues to bear "sick" fruit as it is nourished and vitalized by the negative states of the subject.

All that we call illness, even a purely physical wound like a fractured leg, originates first in the soul.

Nothing happens all by itself; everything has an original cause, a cause which we must always seek in the vibrations of the soul.

The creation of an illness is generally due to psychic and mental states of a destructive character, which have long been within the soul. These negative states form a veritable magnetic nucleus of a highly destructive nature. When one of these electro-magnetic coagulations acquires a great deal of power due to a constant negative state, it unfolds and physically materializes as an illness. This illness, treated by orthodox methods may seem to disappear, but because the root remains within the soul, it can flourish again with the re-occurrence of negative states, which fertilize and feed the tree.

It is also possible that the destructive vibrations which produced the illness penetrated the soul from the outside in a moment of vital weakness or during a strong, depressive or hysterical state, rendering the person's inner defenses vulnerable. That which we call *Aura*, is the electro-magnetic irradiation of an individual and is his protective shield against foreign vibrations. When this defense disappears, the individual is at the mercy of an immense ocean of vibrations from the surrounding atmosphere.

Although it can be argued that many illnesses are caused by germs, one needs to nevertheless consider that the virulence of a germ does not depend exclusively on the germ itself, but on the body's contact with it. The existence of an environment that is receptive to the germ's growth is absolutely necessary. As long as science does not seek the cause of illnesses on the plane of mental energy, it will be impossible to find the principle remedy for these illnesses that are produced by supermicrobes, or etheric microbes which exist as an active principal entirely on the plane of energy. An illness such as cancer could be the result of coming into contact with sick persons while having one's aura open.

These electro-magnetic coagulations can be compared to leeches which settle themselves on parts of the body and begin to suck the vital essence from the cells. Once they have extracted the body's vital essence, cellular degeneration ensues due to a shortage of energy. As the destructive coagulation continues feeding, it becomes stronger and stronger and spreads until it causes total annihilation.

In many cases, illnesses are produced by destructive energetic states generated by the individual himself.

Occult medicine begins therefore, by altering the vibrations of the soul in order to destroy all that is negative which could, or already has, manifested itself as illness. If we could see into the energetic plane, we would be horrified to observe ourselves and others. We would be seeing an animal farm, men with parasites of mental energy embedded in certain parts of their bodies, according to the dominant passion of each individual. Each one of these parasites takes on the form of grotesque animals, real demons which feed on vital energy until complete exhaustion occurs.

It is enough to know that all human energies manifest themselves through the mind, heart and desires, in order to understand that with each desire and each thought we bring to life invisible children which form our good or bad luck. It is for this reason that one can affirm without exaggeration, that man is the child of himself, because he shapes and creates himself in accordance with his energetic formations. It depends on him whether he creates angels or demons.

There are times when we meet people who, despite their clean and well-put-together-look and seemingly normal physical appearances, produce in us feelings of disgust and repugnance, without our understanding the reasons for our reaction.

The reason for such sudden antipathy or sympathy is rooted in the displacement of our vital electro-magnetism, which is produced by the predominant vibration of the other person. This predominant vibration is a result of the union of the individual's thoughts and feelings.

The one who acts according to the laws of Nature is always protected by her, but the one who breaks Nature's laws, must suffer the consequences of Nature's disapproval.

Can the person who takes advantage of any occasion to slander and constantly offend others, complain about his bad luck?

Can the vice-ridden, the drunkard or the depraved complain? Or the pessimist who complains all day and imagines a thousand different calamities?

If we accustom ourselves to carefully analyzing our actions, we will little by little discover the causes for our failure, be it economic, emotional or of any other nature. We will realize that our present situation is a result of a chain of events which stems from negligence, laziness or bad decisions.

The habit of proposing to do many things and of never achieving any, for example, is highly pernicious, because in order to attain mastery and power over outside events, it is first necessary to keep one's word, to fulfill and put into practice one's own decisions. One who practices this precept methodically and patiently will find that his mastery over the forces of Nature increases daily until he is able to fulfill all that he promises to do.

Chance ceases to exist when a man's will is accepted as a law of Nature.

The first step toward the solution of any problem is optimism. It is enough to believe that something can be done to have half the battle won. A positive mental attitude is indispensable for the one who seeks to excel. At each moment, one must feel happy, positive, full of life and energy, and in harmony with the divine creative forces. One must admire beauty in all its manifestations in order to purify and lift one's soul, never feeling conquered or depressed by anything. As the child of God, man has a right to enjoy the protection of his Father and of all His wealth.

By adopting a positive mental attitude, the individual separates himself from all the destructive vibrations that could assail him from without, and in accordance with the law of harmony, he will only capture those vibrations which are positive and uplifting.

Surrounding all towns and cities, is a tangible electro-magnetic "cloud" in which are gathered the instinctive, psychic and mental vibrations of their inhabitants. This cloud floats over these places at a height determined by the density of the vibrations. All those living under it, or all those who arrive there for the first time, absorb the vibrations from this cloud. Unfortunately, we live in a passionate and selfish environment and it is easily understood why we are overloaded daily with undesirable forces. These passionate vibrations of the collective soul of the inhabitants of the city, are those which grab us and submit us to misery, depression, anguish and mediocrity. It is difficult to raise our emotional and mental vibrations above the predominant tone of a social group, but it is the only way to become free of the invisible intoxication produced by these negative forces.

If we wake up some days in a bad mood and say something like, "everything is against me, life is not worth living," we immediately descend to a negative or lower wavelength.

Because we all go through moments of crisis and difficult situations, we must train ourselves *to consciously deny that which is negative or bad for us*. The act of exerting our will and of placing ourselves above everything that is disagreeable or bad for us, is practicing in a scientific way, *mental transmutation*.

This is what it means to act differently from other people who, as soon as they suffer the slightest setback, exaggerate their situation tremendously, by recounting to everybody the "terrible misfortune" they have suffered.

The correct attitude is to keep calm and to vibrate on the opposite pole of the vibration that we wish to change.

Nothing happens by chance in life; everything

occurs as a result of a precise motive or cause. What happens is that we cannot always distinguish the true causes of that which we experience as effects. The law of Cause and Effect is what determines the path we will travel during life and it is therefore quite possible to put into motion only those positive forces or causes that will enable us to reap in the future what we have sown.

The "good or bad luck" of an individual is always due to unknown causes which manifest themselves as effects.

Luck is a question which worries only those abandoned by fortune and by those who have not succeeded in spite of their brave efforts to go ahead.

These unfortunate people look with envy upon those who succeed financially or who are favored by Nature and who seem to have achieved success without any great effort.

Let us carefully examine this point, as it is extremely interesting for those who wish to succeed, because it is only just that man should seek material and spiritual prosperity.

There are four principle factors that determine the "luck" of an individual:

1. His destiny, that is, the position of the stars at the moment of his birth.

2. The destiny of his parents, which in essence is transmitted to the children.

3. His experiences up till 21 years of age, and until he reaches his 33rd birthday.

4. His love life.

We will not consider here mental attitude, will power or other qualities which influence or depend in some way on the factors mentioned above.

1) DESTINY:
From the first moment of life, that is, with the first breath, a child receives cosmic vibrations resulting from the different planetary positions. Each planet has a special electro-magnetic displacement and according to its position in space, it produces different combinations of cosmic rays which govern the future destiny of the child.

Apart from this, we need to consider the amount of *Karma* (causes), either good or bad, that a person carries from previous incarnations which inevitably manifests itself as effects.

If the karma is heavy, it will be difficult to succeed in life until it has been completely expiated. It is possible through Occultism, to change an unfortunate destiny into a successful one, but these truths are for a higher teaching which can only be disclosed to those who embrace the path of initiation.

Many times destiny alone seems to be the only cause of apparent injustices and contradictions in life, when it condemns a being of exquisite sensitivity and intelligence to a life as an outcast, while others living a purely animal existence are favored with material prosperity.

As a result of the supreme law of Cause and Effect, children are born blind, deformed, paralyzed and mentally weak, while others die months or days after having just arrived into this world. There is no injustice, however. Each experiences the effects of actions he has put in motion. God punishes no one. It is man who, by breaking the laws of Nature, punishes and limits himself.

2) INFLUENCE FROM THE PARENTS:

From the moment when an ego (spirit) is in the maternal womb, it begins to receive the electro-magnetic vibrations of the mother through the umbilical cord. If the mother is a passionate, selfish and hysterical woman, these forces will be deeply engraved upon the child. In order to succeed, the child will have to fight the destructive vibrations which were passed on to him. On the other hand, at the moment of sexual orgasm, the father passes on all his spiritual masculine force, which will be the active force that the child will inherit during life. If the father is timid, weak willed and not very virile, the child will always lack the drive or masculine force necessary to succeed in life.

Again, it is relevant to repeat what was stated in the chapter on sex, about the real crime that is committed by engaging in sexual relations once a woman has become pregnant. This factor strongly influences the nervous balance of the future being and therefore affects its destiny.

Other decisive factors are the mental, instinctive and emotional states of the parents at the time of conception, because at that moment, they both form a concrete mold within which the future personality is cast.

It is true that the sins of the fathers are visited upon the children, because in reality, the child is the revelation or continuation of the parents, inheriting in part their karma.

In spite of great scientific advances, the process of procreation is still on a level similar to that of animals as neither the father nor mother can ensure for the child they have created, a life according to the most just and noble human aspirations. They do not know if the child will be normal, if he will be of average intelligence, if he will be healthy or successful in life and other more or less important things. Being born, therefore, is entirely a question of chance. In many cases it means bringing a child into a life of pain, tragedy, illness and misfortune. Does anyone have the right to run a risk of this magnitude? Does anyone have the right to transfer his own sins to a being coming into the world? When science has advanced sufficiently to recognize the truth of what is being said here, the procreation of children will be done scientifically, based upon precise dates and times, in order to produce a race of stronger, more intelligent and more capable beings in all aspects, without the aid of chemical, genetic or biological experiments, but by using the sources we all carry within us and which are close at hand.

3) THE FIRST EXPERIENCES:

From the first breath, the first feeding and the first kiss, different reflexes and habits are imprinted upon the child. In the early stages of life, the foundation of the future man is being laid. A child is like a blank magnetic tape, upon which his experiences are recorded in an orderly fashion. Each of these experiences is yet another brick in the building of the adult. Each positive or negative experience conditions his psyche, giving it a certain form. According to this psychological shape, the adult can succeed or fail. Failure is only a mental state, a product of obstacles which are complexes and inhibitions. This period of first experiences is the one in which there is the greatest risk, because one's future destiny is being formed, that is to say, that forces are being put in motion that will ultimately produce certain effects.

Nothing is more dangerous or decisive than the first sexual experience, because it is what marks the awakening of consciousness. If a woman's first sexual experience is unpleasant, happiness in love will be difficult because she has been psychically scarred. In the same manner, a man's future path will be influenced by the quality of that first sexual experience. When a person's psyche contains a great number of negative factors, it is necessary, through the use of mental power, to cleanse the brain of all the negative recordings, replacing them with positive ones.

One cannot go beyond the limit of one's knowledge and experience: that is, at no time can one react or analyze something from a point of view which is foreign to one's experience and knowledge. However, one who cultivates himself spiritually, may analyze everything from a higher vantage point, because the spirit is beyond good and evil, beyond personality and "points of view." Spirit is essence, life, truth, wisdom and love.

For the student of Occultism, it is entirely possible to change undesirable psychic recordings for others more in tune with his personal aspirations.

4) LOVE LIFE:

The man who has given his heart to a passionate, domineering and hysterical woman, will never be able to succeed in life while still joined to her. When a woman is domineering and does not surrender spiritually to her mate, she absorbs all his etheric masculine magnetism, rendering him empty and depolarized, incapable of creating and forging his path by means of his active force. This man is in a situation like that of a vehicle with a powerful motor which lacks the necessary combustion. This kind of man will always be a failure and if he attains anything, it will be with much sacrifice and only at the moment when the woman is so saturated with his vital energy that she cannot absorb any more from him.

As this woman acquires masculine magnetism, she will become more domineering and imposing in every moment. As it is known, women represent Nature for men. Therefore Nature will react toward man according to the treatment he has received from his woman. If, in an attack of rage, she insults him or shows feelings of hate and jealousy, she will be provoking all that is negative, passionate, deadly and dark upon him, and he will never succeed as bad luck will follow him.

The complete opposite occurs when a man finds a woman who knows how to love, who will surrender herself to him spiritually and who will never, even in an intense moment, react violently towards him, and who will be at his side in sickness and in health, fortune and misfortune. The lucky man who finds a woman with these qualities will be favored by fortune; his lucky star will shine and he will be successful in all his endeavors.

In a woman's case, if she is joined to a weaker man with strong instinctive vibrations, she will always remain limited in her aspirations.

In addition to the four points mentioned which

determine good or bad luck, we will also analyze the relations that maintain the family unit. When there is disharmony, indifference and a lack of cohesion in a family, each member battles life alone, and one who is alone, is at the mercy of the blind forces of Nature, and therefore will be unable to fulfill his aspirations. If the family lives and works solidly united, its members will be on the road to the fulfillment of great accomplishments. If the student does not have this family unity, any collective movement where there is union, fraternity and mutual assistance can fulfill this condition for him. A movement of this nature can be a powerful, yet invisible, help.

That which has been exposed so far can open the door for those who wish to further investigate the causes which determine their luck, because we have given some of the keys to decode these mysteries.

MAGICIANS AND SPIRITISM:

It is necessary to warn those who frequent magicians or fortune tellers in order to learn about their future or to receive promises of wealth or love. These charlatans are veritable accumulators of highly dangerous magnetism emanating from the passional desires of their clients. Through these fortune tellers, "astral shells," or the animal part which survives for a certain time after death, manifest themselves. These beings only seek their own survival, feeding on the flow of energy produced by the emotions of others. These "shells" entangle those seeking advice in a web of lies and bad advice which in the end cause them harm.

potency and origin of that divine force which converted the beast into man.

Many people feel unfortunate, misunderstood or displaced and complain that they are misunderstood by others, that nobody helps them and that others show them only indifference. Good human relationships are impossible between egoists who seek to convert the rest to their own ways of being. These people wish to receive everything — friendship, understanding, love and help, but never do they think to start by giving understanding, help and love. One who is indifferent to the problems of others, will only reap indifference; the egoist, egotism. He who hates, will reap hatred. On the other hand, he who loves, will be loved by his neighbor according to the intensity of his feelings. It is important to know to whom one should offer friendship and trust as there are people who, being morally and spiritually rigid themselves, not only do not repay what they have received, but instead cause harm. The aphorism which reads, "do good to each and every person," should be changed to "do good, but be careful to whom."

Those who are disillusioned with life, skeptical and embittered will find new life and will be spiritually and intellectually renewed if they contribute to works which would benefit others. Health, vigor, youth and beauty are qualities of the soul; they are the manifestation and physical evidence of its balance and energy. Everything that comes to pass, finds its explanation in the mind, as it is there where changes that become evident in the physical body are initiated.

TENSION AND RELAXATION:

Nervous tension is one of the great enemies of psycho-physical equilibrium. Modern life is so frantic, variable and ever changing that the individual must make a tremendous effort to keep up with circumstances. Rapid scientific and social changes produce a state of great insecurity. At a certain point, the repeated efforts to face those changes become so strenuous that they produce exhaustion with all its well known symptoms of nervous tension, irritability, insomnia, digestive disorders, anxiety and anguish, etc.

We will give some general guidelines to help those who suffer from tension.

First of all, it is most important to put the activities of one's daily life into a methodical order, because one of the main causes of tension, is the impatience or anxiety resulting from trying to solve all one's problems simultaneously. Developing patience is essential to being able to relax. There is an excellent exercise that can help in this endeavor. Take twenty matches and put them into a pile on a table. With the left hand, transfer them one by one, to the other side of a table. The only thought at that time should be on what is being done, without any other distraction. This exercise can be done daily. It provokes a state of relaxation and should be done when one is very restless.

Impatience and tension always go hand in hand. Generally, the impatient one is constantly thinking of matters which do not require immediate attention, but which will arise in the near future. This individual lives in a state of anguish which prevents his thorough concentration on the present moment. This bad habit produces a tremendous waste of nervous energy, because the psycho-physical unity is divided by trying to face two problems simultaneously. It is most important to be able to develop the adequate power of concentration, through the training of one's attention and the ability for observation.

During the day, it is very important to establish certain periods of relaxation, endeavoring to remain completely inactive, both physically and mentally. Relaxation can be achieved by deep breathing, loosening the muscles and relaxing when exhaling.

Studying the different positions of the body, it is also possible to establish what causes tension and fatigue. Walking with the spine bent for example increases fatigue, as the center of gravity of the individual is displaced. In addition, sudden uncoordinated and instinctive movements also waste a large amount of energy.

Preparing a specially decorated room for the sole purpose of relaxation, could aid in this endeavor. Soft colors, furniture with rounded contours, soft carpets, sound insulation and indirect lighting should be used. It is then possible, using the Hermetic Principle of Vibration, to create an atmosphere of peace and quiet, filling the atmosphere with mental vibrations which produce this effect.

Other causes of tension which are more difficult to overcome are the psychological conflicts that stem from emotional and instinctive complexes and problems which, for as long as they remain unsolved in the conscious mind of the individual, impede the attainment of true psycho-physical equilibrium. Since the cause of these problems is rooted in the subconscious, daily life will flow along smoothly until the moment in which these problems unexpectedly manifest themselves as neurotic symptoms. In many cases, psychiatric treatment is of great help. In other cases, which are more serious, only a master occultist, profoundly knowledgeable in the secrets of the mind, could be able to disintegrate these negative focal points by means of a complete transmutation of the personality. The initiated master incorporates within himself, the psyches of his patients, purifying them of all scoria with his electro-magnetic influence. Extreme cases such as inversion or insanity, can be cured by this method. A true master must be able to penetrate into the deepest subconscious levels of his students to discover the true causes of all their problems.

THE ROAD TO HAPPINESS:
Many readers who begin the study of

Occultism, will probably feel disconcerted upon realizing that I present it as the sole remedy for all evils. I must call attention to the fact that Occultism is the study of the essence and origin of life, the study of mankind and his complex relationship with Nature and the Universe. By the mere fact that man carries within him the divine spark, he also has latent within him the realization of all possibilities. To unite himself to this divine spark, is to reach the heavens and attain the only true happiness. Real happiness cannot exist when there is no peace within. And who can boast of having this? Who can maintain total calm in the face of life's sudden changes of fortune?

This internal peace cannot be bought with all the riches in the world nor with a title of any kind. A homeless beggar may be happier than a millionaire who lives in a palace.

Being happy is an art that one must study very carefully. This art lies in the ingenious and childlike ability to enjoy things in their natural form; to enjoy a sunset, the fresh morning air, the song of the birds and the contemplation of Nature; to marvel at the multiple forms of life which emanate from God's inexhaustible creative power; to enjoy the simple things within our reach and not to yearn beyond unattainable and grandiose horizons. For the awake and conscious man, a short walk can be the most wonderful adventure. To feel alive, to exist, to be! To feel life flowing through one's veins, the impulse of nervous currents, the heartbeat, the creative power in one's hands. To see and feel the corpuscles of life which float in the air, the scent of life, the warmth of human consciousness, the breathing of the planet, the emotions and thoughts encountered by fellow men, the constant and powerful pressure of the divine spirit, the intelligent power of each organ of the body which fights and strives to keep alive; to be in contact with these, to help them, is to be the lord and captain of one's own small universe. This is being alive, being awake, being conscious.

The intelligent regenerative power which maintains life in the human body tires and becomes exhausted when the mind does not cooperate and give its support. When an individual lives imprisoned by dark thoughts, he tends toward psychic disintegration which greatly influences a vital breakdown. Old age is a progressive defeat of the creative forces by way of a destructive or disintegrating energy. Because the mission of the creative power is to maintain life, the disintegrating force must destroy all that is old, worn out and stationary in order to create new forms of life. Life works for death and death for life. Both are different extremes of that same unique power we call the mind. If we harbor destructive thoughts, we are aiding the process of destruction; that is, we are slowly committing suicide.

It is for this reason that old age begins in the

soul. It begins with the abandonment to a life of ease, idleness, sorrow, sadness and deception. Life is movement and activity. For the one who has led a very active life and who suddenly retires, idleness exiles his creative power and he fades rapidly, like a plant which dies for lack of water and sun. All those who consider themselves old, should try to keep their souls young by seeking new horizons, by keeping alive their youthful illusions, by having faith in humanity and by enjoying the beauty of the world and life. If it is possible, they should fall in love again to rediscover love. As the years go by, love in marriage becomes purely habitual; a couple gets so used to one another that their union is only based on mutual need. However, this is not the love they felt when they first met; the freshness, optimism, life and beauty has disappeared. They should endeavor to find each other again, through courtship and charm, seeking many different ways to surprise and flatter one another. The human soul has so many varied facets that surely there must still be so much to discover about each other. Life resides in change; stagnation and lack of mobility cause death.

Overeating is also one of the main factors of premature old age. By submitting the digestive system to excessive work, its native occult intelligence ends in fatigue. Whoever wishes to prolong his youth should undergo periodic fasts, either total or partial. The secret of life is the alternation of activity and repose. A good example of this is the heart which beats more than 100,000 times per hour.

Pertaining to spiritual perfection, there are many opinions regarding nourishment; some insist that to attain spiritual purity, it is essential to abstain from eating meat. The truth is that there are no general rules as far as this is concerned as everything depends on the constitution of each individual. Some people need meat to maintain their vital energetic level, but for others, eating meat lowers the quality of their mental functioning. Some meat, like pork for example, has an especially low and heavy vibration, and eating it considerably reduces mental agility. This can be verified by analyzing the psychology of those nations which consume large quantities of pork.

Alcohol taken in excess, noticeably lowers the level of consciousness, and tobacco produces the atrophy of certain sensitive brain centers which are also related to consciousness.

The great specter of death does not frighten anyone who has elevated his way of perceiving things. Through comprehension and the practical investigation of life's secrets, a person understands that death is only the beginning of a new form of life. Certainly, birth on the physical plane is more painful than birth on the energetic plane.

For the true occultist, death only signifies the

shedding of one wrapping, to continue life in the invisible world and to return to earth in due course.

Anyone who genuinely feels spiritual restlessness and who meditates profoundly on these concepts will know with certainty the road that he must follow.

PART TWO

Practical Instructions for Attaining
Material and
Spiritual Perfectioning

CHAPTER X

THE DOMINION OF ONESELF —

THE CONQUEST OF ONE'S OWN UNIVERSE

The practical realization of occult teaching begins with the conquest of oneself because all those who want to unveil the secrets of Nature to change their destiny, must fight a battle with themselves until they are victorious. This means to "find oneself," as the "I" generally remains unknown and in the shadows. Within the individual, innumerable tendencies, desires and emotions arise which split his personality, causing him to appear to be both complex and fickle, acting and reacting according to the outside influences which continually occur in his life. The fact of living in a material body creates a perpetual struggle between what the spirit or "I" desires and what the body or mass desires. This struggle always ends with the dominion of the body over the spirit. This situation grows more serious with the identification that is produced between the "I" and purely organic sensations. "I am hungry" or "I am sleepy" refers exclusively to bodily states which reflect in the "I" and oblige it to proceed according to those sensations.

The "I" is like a person who is pulled in various directions at the same time. Consciousness cannot exist when the "I" is dominated by rival forces which push it where it does not desire to go.

If we wish to be conscious, we must conquer our instincts, feelings and emotions, so that the "I" will be the master at all times, not the slave.

It is not unusual to encounter individuals who act against their own principles and wishes, because the "I" at these precise moments was dominated by a powerful inferior force. Given that the body is our concrete manifestation, both visible and tangible, we are the ones who put into order its complex factory in which each workman controls the owner or the employer. Our body is a miniature universe wherein each organ represents a planetary body, acting for the benefit of an intelligent All which must be owner and governor.

In order to work towards the unification of all the energies under the mandates of the "I," it is essential to have a permanent and stable center of gravity, that is, an ideal to aspire to here on earth, similar to the relationship of a root to a tree.

One who has no ideals gambles with his desires, instincts and emotions creating complete chaos in his small universe or microcosm.

If we carefully observe and examine ourselves, we will realize the incredible influence that our states of mind have, and how these then condition our actions.   These psychic states are produced by whatever good or evil penetrates our minds.   In other words, we are a species of slaves to chance.

The many influences that we receive condition our psychic state either positively or negatively.   The subconscious is a fertile ground which conceives all kinds of seeds, whether good or bad.

Parallel to the influences received from the outside, there are the desires which are born within the physical mass or body, whose only concerns are with their own satisfaction and pleasure.

The passions dominate man to a greater or lesser degree according to his spiritual evolution and inevitably lead him to goals never desired by his real and only "I" or spirit.   A man dominated by passion is neither conscious nor intelligent and descends to the level of an animal guided only by its instincts.   It is difficult, nevertheless, to distinguish between the passions and the desires of the "I" and this can only be attained by careful self-observation.

Passion, as the word indicates, is a passive state in which the individual acts out the feminine role, that is, of conceiving within his soul a desire which was received from the outside as a vibration, but which later becomes manifest as a desire that seems to have been born within himself.

A high percentage of what is desired and accomplished by an individual as if they were his own, are fields of vibrations which have penetrated from without and that were born of his physiological self which of course does not represent his "I" in any way.

Due to the fact that the physical body is the dwelling place of the "I," there is constant conflict between the will of the body and that of the spirit. Far from being the master of the material vehicle it has chosen, the "I" is unknowingly converted into its slave, because it is incapable of controlling the four intelligences that work physiologically within the individual. These are the four intelligences of the procreative, digestive, circulatory and respiratory systems.

The procreative system is related to all that is creation; the digestive, with maintaining the physical body; the circulatory, with the emotions, and the respiratory, with the intellect. All that man desires or strives for is manifested through one of these systems, either because it originated therein, or because it penetrated from without. These four intelligences form what we might call the *soul*, or passive side, in contrast to the spirit which manifests itself as the active force.

It is impossible to reach what one desires if the "I" does not hold the reins of power and acquire respect from the body and its different manifestations.

It is very common to observe people in daily life who yearn to achieve something and who formulate elaborate plans of action for attaining their goal but no matter how hard they strive, they are not capable of going straight for their goal as they had desired. Why does this happen? Because an individual is constantly changing.   Every five minutes there appears within him a new personality which does not have the same opinion as the previous one and which insensibly dissuades him from his proposed goal.

We could compare man and these forces to an army without a general, but with many officers, each giving contradictory commands. The soldiers are confused and do not know whom to obey and end up fighting among themselves. The "I" should act as a general with his army and impose its will at all times, so that the fight will be fruitful and not futile, as happens to many in their daily lives who fight powerfully and tenaciously, but who unfortunately do not achieve the desired result. It is essential therefore to establish order in our physical body.

In the first place, it is necessary to be attuned to the constructive forces within the body. We have stated in previous pages that there are two main forces which act throughout the entire universe, and therefore within man; and these are the vital or constructive forces, and death or the destructive forces.

There is always a fierce battle within the body between these two forces which endeavor to annihilate each other.

Death manifests itself through all states of depression and anguish which are usually present. The different names for these states are: pessimism, disillusionment, tedium, sadness, anguish, jealousy, hate, etc.

The constructive or vital forces manifest themselves through optimism, love, happiness, faith and self-confidence.

Let us call the destructive force *negative* and the vital force, *positive*.

The negative state is always distrustful of others; it sees only defects and never virtues; it lives in a gray and dark atmosphere produced by its own emotions and thoughts; it believes that the world is all evil, unfriendly and that life is not worth living.

The pessimist lives in a self-created hell. The optimist, or positive person, on the other hand, is always pleased to be alive, is full of good will towards others and always thinks positively.

There are four magic words which contain the *life force* and these are: *faith, hope, love* and *illusion*.

A child in his innocence teaches us an important

lesson. It is necessary to have faith in oneself, in God and in Humanity. Always keep the hope and the illusion alive for a better tomorrow. Love all human beings equally and everything that carries within the divine spark of the Great Creator.

An atheist who believes in no one and nothing except material phenomena, is dead inside and has a petrified soul.

Once the destructive forces have been expelled, it is essential to begin creating a child which will be our *savior*.

This child is called the *intelligent volitive "I."* This "I" will take charge of directing all the forces which act within the human being.

In order to be successful in creating this "I," it is essential to obtain the following:

1. Education and mastery of the sex.
2. Education and mastery of the heart.
3. Education and mastery of the mind.
4. Education and mastery of the soul.
5. *The maturity of the intelligent volitive "I."*

Once the *intelligent volitive "I"* has been fully developed, nothing is impossible for that man, and he is able to set a goal for himself and walk straight toward it, overcoming all obstacles in his path.

Before proceeding towards any goal, a careful analysis should be made of one's defects or vices.

So as not to lose sight of one's ideal or of what one desires to obtain, this analysis should be written clearly and concisely in a notebook, and reread daily. This is how to set a goal and to not lose sight of it at any time.

The most important thing is to attain total and complete mastery over one's self. This objective, which apparently seems very simple, is the master key to all material or spiritual achievement, because it signifies that one realizes that to become conscious is the supreme goal of the human being.   Due to the simplicity of what has just been said, I fear that my readers will not understand this completely and deem it unimportant. In order to clarify this concept, and since we are now in the era of robots and guided missiles, I will make the following comparison: man is a robot created by someone unknown, a robot in which certain fundamental circuits have been implanted such as the instincts of self-protection, reproduction, emotional reactions and cerebral capacities of logic, deduction and analysis.   This robot then developed a tiny spark, which could be called *consciousness*, and which remains inactive and unnoticed in the majority of human beings who use only the robot-like circuits that were implanted. One who cares for and nourishes the little spark of *consciousness* and enables it to develop in a way that destroys these circuits, indeed takes control of the body. He has overcome all human limitations, because he has made himself more human by surpassing some of the limits imposed on the species.

Therefore, one must begin by educating the material body, which has become accustomed to following its own impulses and which reacts against the master like a wild horse saddled for the first time. The body knows that if it does not fight, it will lose its mastery over the "I," which will become its lord and master.

The greatest obstacle in the way of self-mastery is lack of consciousness of the desires which are not born from the "I," the lack of consciousness of self and the lack of consciousness of being. It is necessary to be fully aware of what should be mastered. It simply has to do with learning to distinguish between desires born from the body or born from the spirit. If it is possible, a list should be made of all desires emanating from the body and of those belonging to the "I."

It must be understood that to master something does not mean to kill or suffocate it. Mastery means accomplishing something only when the *intelligent volitive "I"* desires it. Self-dominion means full possession of the physical vehicle or body which is the abode of the spirit. It means that the spirit has fully adapted its vehicle to its needs. Only then does the spirit fulfill the objective which brought it into life, that is, to be able to act upon matter as easily and consciously as it had previously done on its original plane.   Only then is the person able to think seriously of accomplishing any specific tasks.

The physical body for the spirit is a heavy load when it does not respond to the messages and actions that the spirit desires it to undertake; it is like a black veil which limits and clouds the vision. Self-mastery means learning to handle perfectly the complex and extraordinary machinery which is our physical body.

In general, the condition of the human being can be compared to that of an individual who enters a very complicated automobile without knowing how to drive it. The physical body of a man who has neither cultivated nor developed his consciousness, is like an automobile traveling a long distance without a driver.

In order to clearly visualize the spiritual problem of mankind, we will offer the following simile.   The spirit is pure energy of a high vibration which penetrates a material body of a low vibration. All that the spirit tries to exteriorize is lost, like a radio transmitter of a high frequency that has to be retransmitted to a low frequency receiver (the body). Logically, it is impossible for this receiver (the body) to receive anything at all, until its frequency level is increased to that of the transmitter (the spirit).

Within these concepts resides the true meaning of Occultism, stripped of all lies, vagueness and grandiloquence.

What then, is the means of raising the vibration of the body or mass?

This mass is of a low vibration because it is raw material without consciousness which must be stripped of its animal automatism and provided with a consciousness through the mind, giving consciousness to the hands, arms, legs, feet, brain, heart and liver, etc.

In previous pages, we have established that everything is Mind. Through a conscious mind, it is then possible to modify the basic vibration of an organ or limb, projecting and locating one's consciousness within it. For example, does not a painter give complete consciousness to his hands so that they faithfully portray what his mind sees and commands?

The power of the human mind has no limits and the day will come when man will have attained perfect mastery of the mind, enabling him to materialize his thoughts and giving him the ability to achieve *the integration of matter.*

Through his mind he will be able to modify his cellular structure, overcoming old age and death, for the *principle of Mind* is immortal.

One should meditate deeply on what it means *to be conscious and awake.*

CHAPTER XI

The Development
of Consciousness

Basic Premise: MAN IS A MACHINE

Nothing can be accomplished in the development of consciousness if the student does not fully understand the truth of the following statements: *Man is a machine; he can do nothing; he can accomplish nothing; everything happens to him. He has no will power, no freedom of self-determination. He is at the mercy of the law of chance.*

From what has been stated in previous pages, the attentive reader already has the basic data to understand his mechanical behavior.

Once an individual has lived this experience, he can begin to take action toward slowly awakening himself and emerging from the dreamlike or mechanical state. Naturally, for an isolated man, it is difficult to emerge from a dreamlike state and become conscious, because he soon after falls asleep again and has no points of reference for knowing whether he is asleep or awake. This is the greatest difficulty encountered along the road to consciousness, that is, the impossibility of distinguishing between a dreamlike or awakened state.

When a state of awakening is achieved, even for a short period of time, it is possible to differentiate between the two states.

It is possible to love, think, reason and work without being conscious of what one is doing. Man has very few moments of true consciousness. It is possible to realize the fact that one is not awake only at the moment of attaining consciousness. At that moment, an individual feels a sensation of having been absent for a long time and of having suddenly returned.

What contributes to a great degree to the maintenance of the dreamlike state of an individual are his habits, the identification invariably produced between himself and his actions, and that which he perceives through his senses. He forgets himself and becomes identified with sensations and his consciousness forsakes him to become projected toward or identified with the object to which it is attracted. What remains once this process has begun, is just the human machine which does not make its own decisions, nor really think for itself.

The first step towards achieving consciousness, involves systematic and constant self-observation, to prevent these flights of consciousness. The individual should maintain a constant sensation of his own identity, always thinking, "*I* am the one who wants this; *I* am the one who is acting at this moment; *I* am seeing this." To be conscious, it is necessary to remember one's self, because at the moment of forgetting, the dream state begins.

As it is necessary to perform many activities of a material character, one's own identity is inevitably forgotten. To overcome this obstacle, it is necessary to train one's attention in order to set up a division; in the first place would be the "I," and in the second place, the goal to be attained. This is similar to the beam of a lantern which has to pass through a magnifying glass in order to illuminate an object. The shining beam represents the attention, and the lens, the "I." By means of this analogy it is possible to appreciate the mental technique which is necessary to employ in order to be conscious or awake. Naturally this is only the first step, as there are many degrees of consciousness which one reaches only after successive awakenings.

Once the student begins to try to "remember himself," he realizes how difficult it is, by remembering that a month before he was completely asleep in spite of believing the contrary. Suddenly, and due to some shocks, he awakens and recognizes his previous state of unconsciousness.

When a duality of attention has been attained, it

is necessary to refuse to be identified with emotional states and strong impressions. It is possible that an individual can be conscious in solitude, but upon entering the outside world, he falls into a deep sleep.

In the moments that one receives a strong impression, it is necessary to exert will power to maintain the sensation of the "I." With practice, this becomes very easy. As a more elevated state is attained, a change in perception occurs and things are seen as they are, and not as the individual believes them to be.

Little by little, surprising discoveries are made, such as the discovery that a human being can nourish himself in different ways, the densest of which is digestion and the most subtle, the absorption of energy through stimuli received through the senses. One's scale of values changes completely when one perceives the difference between reality and illusion.

To know where the road to awakening leads, it is necessary to travel upon it, since it is useless to talk about it to one who has not made the journey.

Observe that the spiritual disciplines of the many different philosophical and religious systems all converge on this point. They try to provoke awakening by means of repetition, penance or complicated exercises. From the point of view of consciousness, nothing is more ominous than the happiness which is based solely on the pleasures of the body. All states of sensual pleasure sink those who experience them into a deeper sleep, whereas pain, be it physical or moral, violently shakes the individual, snatching him from his habitual dullness created by his routine, habits and confused mental life.

When man is deeply asleep, Nature sends pain and suffering to awaken him. He who has not suffered in life has no humanity because he sleeps within his own egoism.

The greatest truths are before our eyes, but we are incapable of seeing them. They lie in the simple, humble and unnoticed things.

It is enough to tell the common person that he is asleep for him to react sarcastically and incredulously. Only one among thousands will be able to give the necessary weight to what this means.

For the common man, evolution, consciousness, will power, self-determination and humanity do not exist. Many will feel an affinity to the ideas presented in this book, but very few will dedicate a serious study to them in order to prove through their own experiences, the truth of what has been stated here.

It is so difficult to understand what it means to be conscious that many will find it hard to accept that it is not always the most cultured or educated who is the most conscious. Consciousness has nothing to do with this. A humble and uneducated gardener may be more conscious than a nuclear physicist. It is necessary to understand that we are speaking of consciousness as the capacity to perceive reality without mental distortions of any kind. In many cases, excessive scientific or cultural information is a serious obstacle for attaining consciousness, as this kind of information originates mainly from "unconscious" individuals and is consequently fragmented, incomplete and unreal. In order to understand this completely, it is sufficient to consider that within one or two hundred years from now, much of what is taught today in universities will surely cause laughter. Scientific knowledge does not lead to wisdom when it stems from an inaccurate basis and may even lead to an erroneous course. It is also interesting to think that scientific laws, which may be established in the future as a result of diverse investigations, already exist today, but in an occult form.

Science only paraphrases occultism, announcing "discoveries" which were known by the Egyptians and the Rosicrucians.

It is important to analyze the relationship that exists between consciousness and the concepts of good and evil. Consciousness is beyond good and evil, as these terms are totally relative. Generally what is good for some is evil for others. One individual may be very loving, and full of love towards others and do all the good he can, but his benevolence may be entirely mechanical and unconscious and a product of cerebral automatism. Another, may be good because his mother ingrained in him kindness, or because he adopts a "pose" in order to feel superior and thus neutralize an inferiority complex. This type of love, kindness and charity is relatively easy to find, but true love, authentic, genuine and conscious love towards others is extremely difficult to find.

One who reaches consciousness, is in tune with divine law and is in harmony with the irradiation of the great universal Mind or God.

"Ask and ye shall receive" was said over two thousand years ago by Jesus, the Christ, the super-conscious son of the great universal Mind (the Virgin).

Few have been able to understand this teaching, as everything said by this great master has been falsified, misinterpreted and capriciously explained. *When one who is in harmony with God, asks for something from the depths of his heart, his petition is similar to an order from God himself and must come to pass sooner or later.*

But, can one be considered conscious if one lives enslaved to the sensual intoxication of matter? Can the one who amasses wealth without any thought toward others, be conscious?

Let us recall another aphorism of Jesus Christ: "Give and you shall receive."

One who wishes to receive, must start by

giving, both in business as well as in human relationships. One who is more concerned with satisfying his clientele than with filling his pockets, will always receive just compensation for his deeds. One who gives friendship, will receive friendship. One who understands others, is understood and tolerated. There are people who complain bitterly of loneliness, lack of friends and of not being understood. This type of person never stops to think that it is not right to request understanding from others, as this is equivalent to asking everyone to adjust and condition their ideas to his, and this is not possible.

One must begin by tolerating and understanding others, tolerating their defects and imperfections. All have within them the essence of love towards others, but the great majority have not reached into themselves to reveal this love.

One who is, or who has started to obtain consciousness, must learn to live according to the laws of Nature which are the forces that are manifested by God so that life may exist.

Even a very conscious person cannot break these laws or try to go beyond them, but he can and must, use them consciously for the benefit of humanity.

One of these laws is the law of "the survival of the fittest."

One who desires to accomplish something must make himself strong so that he is not swept away by others stronger than he.

Because we act within a physical body, we must start by keeping it in a perfect state of health.

One of the most important factors for perfect health is the careful avoidance of negative emotions such as depression, melancholy and sadness, as these provoke a loss of vital energy.

If it is true that these psychic states may be due to purely physical causes, then the change that occurs in the health of an individual who begins to think or feel positively, is significant. The mind must be taught to think for itself about pleasant things, eradicating all that is evil, useless and a waste of time.

Moderation in food is fundamental to avoid lowering excessively the volitive vibration, as all ingested matter lacks consciousness and must be assimilated and digested by the stomach and by the consciousness.

Always keep active, doing physical exercises according to one's age and physical constitution.

Do not smoke or drink alcohol. The cigarette is a slow but sure way to sap creative faculties.

Complete and deep breathing helps enormously

to maintain physiological equilibrium and increases one's resistance against illness and nervous depression.

It is important to understand that complete breathing begins by taking air into the stomach, then into the diaphragm and then into the chest. Exhalation must be as complete as possible.

It is also recommended to stand before an open window every morning and to breathe deeply for five or ten minutes, with the mind concentrated on what is being done.

Once energy has been obtained from food, sleep and deep breathing, it is necessary to learn to economize this energy.

The true occultist should manage his own energy perfectly. He should know exactly how to distribute and organize it, so as not to squander it, which is what usually happens.

In order to be able to distribute vital energy correctly and perfectly, it is most necessary that thoughts and actions should follow the same course. It is extremely damaging to constantly think about what has to be done in the next ten minutes or half hour. This bad habit is one of the principal causes of anxiety and manifests itself in the form of extreme impatience to finish everything rapidly and to reach the end of the road. One who suffers from this chronic anxiety lives mentally projected into the future.

It is interesting to analyze the disastrous effects which are produced by the squandering of energy, such as a lack of interest and enthusiasm to achieve anything.

The simple act of picking up a coin off the ground, if done indifferently and without the desire to do so, consumes more nervous energy than running 100 meters with enthusiasm. In all books dealing with psychology, we read that enthusiasm is one of the most powerful forces in existence. What is the reason for this power?

Enthusiasm is a state of profound spiritual exaltation which produces perfect mental and psychic concentration.

Within this message, lies the key to maintaining a constant flow of energy. Let us make an effort to accomplish our daily labor with as much enthusiasm as if our lives depended upon it. Even the simple and routine act of shaving or dressing, for example, should be done enthusiastically and with interest.

One who cannot burn with enthusiasm for something, will never be triumphant. It is not sufficient to wish to triumph, nor enough to wish to win; it is necessary to feel within oneself *a profound and sustained thirst* for accomplishing what is desired. All desires and energy should be concentrated on what one wants to attain, because one who desires a thousand small things at once obtains nothing, for he disperses his mental power in all directions.

There are three things that are intimately related and which must be used together to develop consciousness; imagination, feeling and action or movement of the body.

Walking, working with one's hands and movement in general, powerfully influence the mental and emotional states of the one who carries out these activities.

On the other hand, the quality of one's thoughts and emotions also influence the way one moves, speaks and walks.

It is interesting to realize that through the body's movements, we are able to affect the soul in order to modify negative states, replacing them with superior vibrations. This is the reason for certain movements and signs of Catholic, Masonic and other such disciplines.

A man who is strong, optimistic and psychically healthy walks upright, head lifted, shoulders held back and gives an impression of confidence and strength in all his movements. When he shakes hands, his grip is strong and decisive and his voice is firm and clear. One who is nervous walks bent over, never looking straight ahead nor talking in a group, and if he does so, his voice noticeably trembles. This man should practice "psychic vitalization" as stated in this book, in order thus to become a conqueror.

To change a negative mental and psychic state for a higher state, the following exercise can be done to successfully produce calmness, peace and serenity.

- Strive to reduce the speed of what you are doing until movement is like a slow motion camera.

- Every movement should be carefully studied and must be done with concentration, with "the soul" in it. Breathe deeply and relax all the muscles.

This exercise produces a deep state of mental concentration which is difficult to reach by other means.

During this exercise it is very important to feel or to be conscious of every part of the body that is in motion. Once this has been attained through practice, the muscles, nerves, blood and the air entering into the lungs must be felt.

Naturally this procedure should be adopted only during the exercise. At night, when preparing for bed all muscles should be relaxed in order to sleep more deeply than usual. Generally, profound sleep is not attained until there is a total muscular and nervous relaxation which may take up to three to four hours. Generally speaking, we do not experience the effects of

energetic rejuvenation during this period we call pre-
or preparatory sleep since this renewal takes place
only during deep sleep. Thus, one who is able to enter
rapidly into a deep sleep will keep his body full of
energy and will require less sleep as he takes full
advantage of all his hours of slumber.

In order to relax, follow this procedure: lie
down, breathe deeply several times and calmly
concentrate your thoughts on the solar plexus. Once
this pattern of breathing is established, start by
relaxing the facial muscles, forehead, eyes and jaws,
then continue with the neck, arms and thorax, until
reaching the feet.

In the case of illness, the student should make
an effort to regain his health by using his mental
power. Illness is only a negative vibratory state, and,
as with all vibrations, may be altered by use of mental
power. The speed with which the organism responds
when it feels the support of an intelligent, mental force
that is trying to help it overcome its illness, is
surprising.

The great obstacle that the desire for spiritual
perfectioning comes up against, is inertia or negative
power.

The desire and wish to excel form a powerful
active force in the individual, an active force which is
opposed to one's habitual mechanical life, represented
by inertia.

In order for this active force to not be annulled by one's negative part, the student must constantly fortify it by means of study and rigid self-discipline. The majority of students of Occultism limit their accomplishments to good intentions only, because all their labor swings like a pendulum between the active and negative forces, a situation that may last a lifetime. This is the great danger of being alone and isolated. One who desires to attain spiritual perfection all by himself commits the greatest error, because the sense of peace and tranquility that comes about, is not a result of self-domination, but is a result of the absence of the "psychic shocks" received from other personalities.

This man feels at peace and firmly believes he has found himself and conquered consciousness. He does not realize that his tranquility is born from a deep state of sleep. Thus, just as evolution exists, so does "involution," or retrocession. Therefore the type of spiritual fulfillment of which we have spoken above is involution, because when an individual normally lives among others, he is constantly encountering "psychic shocks" which contribute to keeping him awake. When these shocks disappear due to his isolation in a monastery, for example, deep sleep ensues which naturally offers great tranquility, but not consciousness.

It is for this reason that the ideal condition for achieving true and effective spiritual progress which will lead to consciousness and will power, is to work within a group under the guidance of one who is truly and effectively awake. This guide will constantly endeavor to maintain and produce situations destined precisely to keep his disciples from sleeping, to keep them awake.

CHAPTER XII

EDUCATION OF THE WILL

Apart from intelligence, the most precious gift of the human being is will power. In the great human mass, will power is confused with simple desire.

Will power goes further however, as it is rooted in the depths of one's self. It is a powerful internal "pressure," the visible manifestation of what an individual wishes to accomplish. The expression "to have will power" is very apt, as it refers to a man who imposes on himself a rigid discipline in order to attain a desired purpose.

This power or capacity for self-mastery is manifested in diverse forms in different people. Some have a great deal of this power and others lack it completely. Success in life depends to a great extent on the will power of an individual, on one's capacity to persevere, to work hard when others falter, to overcome unpleasant situations, misery and failure.

There are people of great intelligence and exquisite sensitivity, who cannot forge their way in life because they lack will power.

On the contrary, we see others who are successful, not always for their great intelligence, but whose constancy, absolute dedication to work and strong character help them to overcome all obstacles. Many times a poorly educated, obtuse and insensitive individual is more capable of success than someone who is very cultured and sensitive because he has no fear of injuring others or harassing them with demands of a commercial nature, for example. A very sensitive man, on the contrary, is always wondering what the man he visits for commercial or work-related purposes is thinking of him.

These "considerations" toward others, undermine his "drive" as he is afraid of being ill received and fears that he may be in the way or may become bothersome. The thought of "what will people say" is a sure cause of failure and limitation. One who thinks this way has a passive personality and is therefore unable to impose his will upon those of a positive nature, unless he develops courage, drive, audacity and an absolute lack of "consideration" toward others. It is necessary to understand the sense and the way the word "consideration" is used here.

It is interesting to check the intimate relationship that exists between will power and enthusiasm. One who is able to feel enthusiastic about something is very close to possessing will power. We could say that will power is "contained, sustained and reasoned enthusiasm."

Apathy, or lack of will power is characterized by an absolute indifference toward everything; lack of self love; lack of interest in oneself and in others.

A cold and indifferent person can never influence others to help or support him at any time, because he cannot communicate to them the psychic vibration of enthusiasm; and when we come across someone with a lack of enthusiasm, we think that he is not convinced of the goodness or quality of the product or ideas he wishes to sell. This person cannot sell himself even to himself, and is unable to display his hidden values.

Here are some recommendations for the Education of the Will:

<u>Exercise Plan</u>

- Intense physical exercises, according to the capacity of the student. These may vary from weight-lifting to exercises of any kind. Appropriate exercises which are suitable for any need or age can be found in any physical education manual.

- Five to ten minutes of deep breathing every morning. Stand with arms outstretched to the side upon inhaling, retain your breath as long as possible, and exhale through the mouth, simultaneously and slowly, dropping the arms.

- Sit on a chair with hands tightly clenched, breathe deeply, concentrating upon what you are going to say, and repeat the following in a decided and energetic manner: *"My will is strong and powerful. My will is strong and powerful. My will is strong and powerful. Everything that I desire, I will achieve because I am a center of accumulation of life, strength and power."*

- Sit completely upright in a chair with the spine straight, hands closed tightly, legs together, and remain completely immobile as long as possible. This immobility should be total and complete.

- When completely exhausted physically, upon arriving home to rest, go out again and walk for a few minutes. During this walk mentally repeat, "I am making this sacrifice so my will power will increase daily more and more."

As a general rule for development, the following suggestions are given: Never give way to all the desires that appear during the day. A desire is a powerful force which is extinguished upon the satisfaction of it. If we refuse to satisfy many of these desires, retaining this power and maintaining it in suspense, we have in our hands a powerful energy which increases our personal magnetism.

The physical body is like a horse which must be kept on a short rein to keep it from running away. If we give way, it starts to demand more and is never satisfied. It is necessary to have absolute control over food, alcohol and cigarettes which are strong and constant temptations. Every temptation given into, is strength that is lost. Sleep must be carefully regulated; we must not sleep more than necessary. Upon awakening in the morning, the habit of remaining in a half-awake state or of daydreaming should be carefully avoided as this habit creates disorder in the imagination and subsequently becomes a physical disorder. Avoid as much as possible unconscious and mechanical actions, such as nail biting, tapping on the floor with the foot, swaying when standing up and other actions of a similar nature. Endeavor to stabilize psychic activity, that is, to not change suddenly from laughter to sorrow. Always be tranquil and calm.

In the measure that one begins to manage one's emotions and impulsive actions, a similarly stronger will power will develop, which will easily impose itself upon negative forces or inertia.

One habit which should be developed as much as possible in order to attain strong will power, is order. Draw up a plan of work ahead of time for each day and do not alter or change it for any reason whatsoever.

Get into the habit of always accomplishing what is proposed no matter how small this may be. One who is not capable of making his own decisions becomes a mere toy of Nature.

Feel yourself at all times to be the owner and master of your body, which may be commanded at any moment to execute what is desired.

It is superfluous to state that an individual with vices, whatever these may be, cannot acquire strong will power. Therefore, one who is enslaved by a vice must cut it out at the root or at the cause of it. Vices, bad habits and complexes are veritable chains which completely paralyze will power.

CHAPTER XIII

Education and
Mastery of the Sex

Habitually, man uses his sex in any moment that he experiences erotic desire and does not bother to regulate or organize his creative function.

His sexual instinct exercises such dominion over him that it obliges him to procreate in the moment that this instinct awakens.

This sexual desire is exactly the same as other desires, that is, man identifies with it in a way that has fatal consequences for the development of his consciousness.

Is there anyone who can remain conscious at the moment of orgasm?

It is precisely in the loss of consciousness at that moment that the only sexual "sin" lies, because that which is sexual, like everything else, has its positive and negative aspect. The negative aspect is encountered when the sexual instinct dominates over the will and consciousness. This was the fall of Adam. The positive aspect is seen in a man who is in total control of himself, who uses sex only when his consciousness permits.

One aspiring to excellence must become the master of his sexual instinct so as to channel this into a vibration of purity and spiritual elevation.

When sexual relations are driven solely by instinctive passions which seek only the satisfaction of material desires, there are dire consequences for both lovers as they open up their psyches to purely passional and materialistic vibrations. With the penetration of these vibrations, only seeds of misfortune and unhappiness are sown. All sexual relations which do not consist of the intimate communion of a deep and true love, along with great attraction and spiritual harmony, are useless for spiritual development.

Not only should there be a union of bodies but also a union of the soul and of the spirit.

Sex is the most important factor for good or bad luck in a man because for him, woman represents Nature, the provider of all good things in life. A passionate, hysterical, egotistic and jealous woman brings "bad luck" to a man, because she transmits her discordant vibrations to him and he encounters in life something similar to what she has irradiated. This type of woman does not really love her partner but desires to possess and completely dominate him. With much more frequency than we think, the failure of a man is due to the fact that his woman suffers from the "Diana Complex." Within her is a true sexual disturbance which makes her act like the male on the plane of energy, and her man therefore assumes the role of the female. As a female in a man's body, it will be impossible for the man to be a success in life because he will lack that which is active, that is, radiant masculine magnetism.

A woman, who acts in this way, commits a true sin because she goes against the laws of Nature by losing her femininity, and as a result of this, she will always receive the punishment of Nature in one way or another. This can only be avoided by recapturing her femininity, by means of rigid psycho-sexual discipline. The interchange of psycho-sexual magnetism between men and women involves secrets that are frightening in their scope. These teachings should only be imparted to those who have proven their morality and pure love for Humanity, and who have entered an occult school under the direction of a true Master. This book can only give general guidelines as it is a text for public circulation.

When a man sees that he is pursued by "bad luck" he should carefully examine the quality of the sexual union with his partner and he will easily be able to discover the cause of his problem. The same applies with respect to the woman.

The worst thing that is found to exist in the relationship of a couple is the passionate oscillation that is produced between sexual union and arguments.

A great percentage of intimate relationships follow this sequence: sexual union — argument; argument — sexual union.

If couples only knew how they limit their possibilities with these situations, they would be careful not to fall into this pattern.

Each conjugal argument is a seed of ruin, poverty, misfortune and "bad luck" which fatally materializes when it reaches fruition.

There are women who unconsciously trample on men, smothering them until they are converted into beings without character, beaten down subjects who only obey that which such women impose. This type of woman has a dominant personality that subconsciously wishes to possess even the thoughts of her partner and thus absorb all his etheric-virile magnetism. All timid men are such because their mothers were very domineering or because their wives are tyrants.

The woman who gives herself totally to a man, spiritually and physically, brings him "good luck" and makes it possible for him to succeed.

This woman yearns to give rather than receive; she gives herself completely to her partner, fights for him and is always by his side in difficult moments. She has the necessary intelligence for persuading him without trying to dominate him. The "Diana" wishes to have the man on his knees at her feet; the other type of woman wishes to see him as a superior being with outstretched hands to support her in all ways.

With men, exactly the same occurs, for there are two types: the one who only wishes to have a slave, and the one who desires a real wife, conscious of her true role.

The chauvinist man lacks the moral authority necessary to have a woman give of herself completely.

It is the responsibility of the man to know how to conquer and motivate his companion because all forms of discord are a shared responsibility.

Therefore, one who desires his own spiritual development must regulate his sexual activity according to a preconceived plan, in mutual agreement with his companion.

Times when one must abstain from sexual activity:

When emotionally disturbed, especially after an argument.
After drinking too much alcohol.
When a woman has her menstrual period or immediately after.

When there is no emotional or spiritual attraction.
After visiting a sick person.
When either one is ill.
When a woman is pregnant.

There must be complete tranquility and harmony during the sexual union and the act itself must be surrounded with as much purity and delicacy as possible, carefully abstaining from "embellishments" which inevitably lead to impotence and frigidity. Throughout the entire sexual act, one should have complete possession of oneself without abandoning oneself to animal sensuality.

CHAPTER XIV

EDUCATION AND
MASTERY OF THE HEART

Nothing is more important to an individual's life than his feelings and psychic states as these are the basic vibrations which determine the path taken by him each day. The quality of the individual's magnetic vibrations which manifest during each day, are determined by his psychic states. Unfortunately, our feelings are conditioned to a great extent by the good or bad impressions that we receive in any instant, which when combined with vibrations, give birth to a psychic state. Feelings are very strong vibrations, which may be destructive or constructive. Sadness, melancholia, hate and jealousy are terribly destructive vibrations which may poison the blood to the point of self destruction. It is well known how psychic states influence one's facial expressions, for example, to the point of completely disfiguring the face, under the influence of a negative psychic state. If women only knew that each feeling of sorrow, sadness and depression leaves its mark on their faces, they would carefully avoid such depressive states.

When we meet people whose habitual psychic state is sadness, their vibration is transferred to us and, without knowing why, we feel depressed.

Those who are always in a state of happiness and love, distribute positive vibrations of joy, well-being and tranquility.

Habitually, the human being lives as a slave to his feelings, which impose upon him certain vibratory states to which he must adapt. This particular state of living enslaved to feelings, provokes a noticeable deformation of perception, having produced a distortion of the dominant emotional tone. It is possible to perceive objectively, only when the psychic source has been educated. Due to the great influence of feelings over reason and judgement, it is almost impossible for an individual to judge and evaluate correctly. If we add to this, the influence of the personality, we can see that it is impossible for man in this everyday state to see the truth. Because of this, man makes many mistakes which make it difficult for him to channel his life in the direction he wishes.

There are people who lead unfortunate lives because their psychic states constantly oscillate from the positive to the negative. These unfortunate beings live a tortured existence for they cannot find themselves in any moment, because when they have been able to penetrate one psychic state in order to know themselves, they have already oscillated to the other extreme, resembling a dog who tries to bite his own tail.

Another of the most terrible psychic illnesses is hyper-sensitivity. Those who suffer from this feel hurt and offended by everything. They think everybody sets out to annoy them and that the entire world is conspiring against them. They cannot be joked with because they simply do not understand and they firmly believe that they are being laughed at. Generally, behind this attitude there lies deep egoism. This individual lives within himself and believes that he is the center of the world, and as such, everyone is obliged to serve him, consider, respect and understand him. When he realizes that people do not serve nor consider him as he wishes, he suffers deeply and feels extremely unfortunate, claiming that "nobody understands him" and that he is "alone in the world." He always expects everyone to come to him. In marriage, these kinds of people are extremely unhappy because they expect their partners to relinquish their own lives and individuality in order to live dependent on them.

What leads a person to this kind of state? Possibly, a broken home in which the individual lacked the love of his parents, and who now as an adult, has an exaggerated need for love, care and attention.

There are many deformations of the personality due to unbridled feelings, but all can be corrected by the will directed by *consciousness*.

The heart must be used as a conscious and intelligent organ in order to receive only the most elevated feelings.

In order to attain psychic serenity, extremes of unbridled joy and exaggerated sorrow must be avoided. An attitude of calm, peace and tranquility should reign as the dominant feeling.

Self-possession, courage and *sang-froid* should be cultivated until the heart is strengthened so that nothing can harm or change it and that only with full consciousness will it permit the overflowing of love or joy.

In order to accomplish this, one should frequently meditate, concentrating one's thoughts on the heart and thinking that it is there that total and complete serenity reigns.

Fraternal and Christian love, in the correct sense, are a powerful help towards attaining tranquility. If one is constantly sending feelings of love towards others, unexpected good is done, because upon receiving these vibrations, a similar feeling is awakened in the recipient.

"Love one another" should be practiced in every sense of the word, without distinction of race, class or color.

CHAPTER XV

EDUCATION AND MASTERY
OF THE IMAGINATION

Generally, it is the imagination which completely dominates man, driving him to accomplish everything he sees within it. The imagination, just like the heart, is equally influenced by the constant impressions received from the outside.

The imagination is a kind of mirror which reproduces images based on the information received by the senses. The orders which are given by the brain to be executed as concrete actions, depend upon this image.

The degree of clarity of the mental image that is reflected by the individual's imagination will determine the capacity of the individual to judge either correctly or incorrectly the information received by his senses. When the mental image is blurred, there will be confusion and disorientation because the information received will not be clear.

A lack of clarity in the imagination is generally due to the limitation of the senses which only perceive a narrow range of phenomena.

The most important factor to take into account when considering the imagination, is that it is creative and that an image which is repeated becomes established as a physical, concrete and tangible reality.

For this reason, people become victims of their own wandering imagination because they imagine a thousand different things during the day, completely dispersing their mental power which becomes incapable of accomplishing anything concrete.

How many people constantly bemoan their "bad luck" and bitterly complain of a thousand different ailments which exist only in their minds, thus bringing about, through their imagination, the very situations they have imagined. In the long run, these people face many unpleasant things, and strange and incredible misfortune follows them. It is then that they say: "What have I done that God should punish me in this way?" In their blindness, they do not realize how much they themselves have created their own mishaps. God punishes no one, as he is *all love and kindness.* It is man who, ignorant of the laws of Nature, places obstacles in his own path.

From the point of view of the struggle for existence and for the conquest of good fortune, it is interesting to observe that many individuals, with an impetuous and fertile imagination, live their lives without ever reaching their desired goals. On the other hand, there are those of little imagination and intelligence who are strong and tenacious, and who thus open the road to success and to higher goals. This is because the imaginative individual generally squanders his creative mental power by means of an uncontrolled imagination, and as a result, in the majority of cases, he lacks the mental power necessary to convert his ideas into reality.

It is absolutely necessary to have complete dominion over the imagination and for this, mental concentration, order, calmness and patience must be practiced. The bad habit of letting one's thoughts wander should be completely eliminated, and the practice of thinking only about what one is doing in the present moment needs to be established in its place.

The most important exercise for controlling the imagination is as follows:

Let the mind remain blank for 5 to 10 minutes. Sit or lie in bed and breathe deeply, relaxing all the muscles in the body. Once relaxation is achieved, try to hold back all mental activity until the imagination is totally blank. Breathing is of great help for this, because by lowering the rate of respiration, that is, by breathing very slowly, mental calmness is produced immediately.

CHAPTER XVI

Use of the
Powers of the Mind

Everything is Mind; the Universe is Mental; it is the master key which permits us to understand all of Nature's secrets and to penetrate into the very heart of the *Great Universal Father-Mother*, that is God. Let us consider the mind as the primordial or only energy from where everything is born and to which everything returns. From mental matter, the spirit of man is formed. Minerals are formed from mind; from mind emerge vegetables, planets, galaxies and all that exists in the Universe. Mind is the immortal reality which is hidden behind all appearances. It is the essence of all that exists, be it animal, mineral or human. As a conscious manifestation, it produces the miracle of human thought.

The mind is the most powerful instrument the human being possesses. The strength of his thoughts create in the mental world or on the archetypal plane a thought-form which, if sustained for a sufficient time, materializes in a concrete form. The occultist or mental magician is a man who has learned to manage mind-matter through his thoughts. Just as on the physical plane where we can touch and see all material objects, it is also possible to touch and see thoughts on the mental plane. On the mental plane, a thought is a material object as solid as a rock on the physical plane.

Every person has what we could call his own mental edifice, which is the magnetic field of power built from the sum total of his thoughts during his life. The quality of what an individual encounters in life, depends upon the quality of this mental structure.

A negative thought, albeit fleeting, strongly influences the life of the one who has conceived that thought.

This affirmation will be better understood through the study of the nature of thought, which is similar to radio waves. When one thinks, one emits waves according to what one imagines. We live in a veritable mental ocean or sea of thought waves of diverse types, thoughts which are captured as soon as we place ourselves on their same wave lengths. If, at a certain moment, we have a depressing thought, we tune our mental receiver to the depressive wave length and we capture all depressive thoughts that are vibrating in the atmosphere. Instead of a negative load of ten units, for example, we will have one a thousand times heavier. The importance of having only positive thoughts and of being optimistic in order to absorb positive elements of strength and energy, is thus apparent.

In this chapter, we will give the keys for conscious action on the mental plane, on how to use our powerful mental strength, but these keys will only be understood by those who can read between the lines and who are prepared to see and understand the truth.

If what you aspire to flows toward truth, love and universal well-being and is sufficiently strong, you will be able to contact the invisible planes with the occult power which will guide and channel you toward what you desire.

One who is not prepared to see the truth and penetrate into the sanctuary of *Isis*, will only encounter words, darkness and emptiness.

The mental plane is like the matrix where the seed which penetrates it is conceived and developed. Once a seed is deposited into this gigantic womb it will inevitably develop within a time according to its magnitude.

Nothing is more certain than the popular aphorism which says: "One who sows in the wind will reap the whirlwind."

Take great care not to sow evil thoughts in the Great Mother, as you will encounter pain, desperation and suffering because she conceives everything, both good and evil, and you will reap the fruit of what you have deposited in her.

Emit only thoughts of love, success, well being, abundance and prosperity. Always desire the best for your neighbor.

Never swear or use bad language as in due course these will materialize.

There are certain special conditions for the fulfillment of this act of creation, or marriage between the human mind and mental matter and one of these is that the seed deposited should be fertile.

How to make this seed fruitful is something that each one must discover for himself through meditation, love and service to one's neighbors.

This is the mental power Adam and Eve possessed in Paradise, that is, the capacity to create with their minds everything they desired, a power they lost after eating the forbidden fruit.

The student who wishes to make use of his mental power should remember the following laws: all that we see as tangible phenomena on earth are but manifestations of mental energy at different vibratory states. *Everything vibrates; everything is mind in vibration.* A rock vibrates, an apple vibrates, a feeling is a vibration. Absolutely everything that exists in the Universe is a vibration. The art of having influence over events consists of the adequate handling of vibrations.

Mental transmutation is the true power of the Initiate, the power which permits one to change undesirable vibrations to desirable vibrations.

Hate may be transmuted into love, indifference into interest, cowardice into courage, scarcity into abundance, misfortune into happiness.

Everything can be changed through the transformation of its basic vibrations. From this fact comes the tradition of the alchemical transmutation of lead into gold, a symbol of the transformation of man's animal instincts into spiritual gold.

Each person has a dominant vibration which is like a selector dial that tunes the individual with similar vibrations. One who vibrates pain, will find pain. One who vibrates poverty, will find poverty. One who vibrates illness, will find illness. One who vibrates love, will find love. One who vibrates hate, receives hate. Love and be loved. Hate and you will be hated. Despise and you will be despised.

Meditate constantly upon wisdom, love and truth and you will deserve the true wisdom of the initiate, which is beyond good and evil, beyond life and death, beyond pleasure and pain.

How one thinks determines what one will find in one's path. No one has the right to bemoan his bad luck as each one can become the architect of his own destiny.

Abstain from thoughts about sad, depressing or unpleasant things; fix your mind on everything that is fine and beautiful, on goodness and love. Never criticize your neighbor, never look for defects in others; always endeavor to find good qualities and virtues. Even in the most perverse man can be found something worthwhile. Let us recall what Jesus said when he and his disciples passed by the rotting body of a dog which had a terrible odor; everyone drew back with repugnance, except Jesus, who said, "What beautiful teeth this animal has. They shine like pearls."

If you learn to find gold even in dross, you will have been converted into a true spiritual alchemist.

Criticize a man and you will be tying him down with chains; praise him and you will help him to succeed.

When you need the cooperation of someone in order to accomplish your work, go and visit him with confidence, imagining him as your brother and sending him vibrations of love and brotherhood, and you will be well received.

Everything is within your reach if you learn to use your mind, but beware of abusing this power, of using it to injure others or to obtain material possessions born of greed and ambition.

Nobody has a right to take from the Universal Mind more than he is legitimately entitled to, and one who tries to do so will receive his just punishment.

Before you decide to put into use your mental strength, it is a good idea to meditate deeply in order to ascertain that what is desired is correct and justly deserved.

To mold ideas with strength and power so they may materialize rapidly, it is necessary to be a miser with one's thoughts, to economize one's mental power by keeping the mind blank until the time comes for "mental projection."

You must guard in profound secrecy your projects, because if you speak of them, you immediately provoke a reaction against them.

Never must you doubt the success of your project as doubt is negative and destructive.

You must be patient and endeavor not to pick

the fruit before the necessary time has elapsed for its formation, birth and ripeness.

Once you have obtained what you desire, you must be prepared to face the reaction you will encounter regarding what you have done.

The Principle of Cause and Effect governs all.

All actions provoke reactions of the same magnitude, but in the opposite direction.

This reaction can only be prevented by powerful self-mastery. Let us remember always the Law of Vibration. If we have something and do not wish to lose it, we must polarize ourselves strongly toward what we have obtained, to prevent the reaction from reaching us and wresting from us the fruit of our mental creation. If you are ill, remember that this illness is only an undesirable vibratory state which can be transmuted into a healthy vibration.

Together with the Hermetic Principle of Vibration, the Principle of Correspondence should be used: *"As it is above, so it is below, and as it is below, so it is above."* All that which exists outside man, has its equivalent within him, and therefore, all we wish to accomplish on earth, must first be accomplished within our soul. If this internal accomplishment is achieved, materialization on the physical plane will also be attained.

The magic key to obtaining all that one desires, dwells in the wise application of the magical triangle; illustrated as follows:

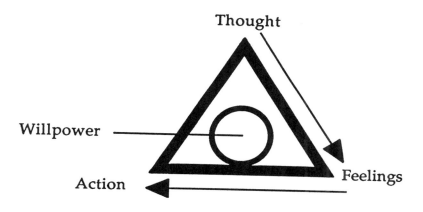

To conclude, I wish to warn that all mental action must be based upon universal harmony, love and goodness. One must never endeavor to obtain what one does not deserve as this is a theft in which the All is the victim and because it is a theft, what was obtained will have to be returned very shortly and the corresponding fine will be levied.

CHAPTER XVII

SEARCH FOR HAPPINESS

Nothing is longed for more by human beings than happiness. Yet how many can say that they are happy? Certainly, only a small and select minority of the human race has acquired the precious gift of happiness.

The search for happiness is constant and never ending, and leads each individual to try in his own way, and by different paths, to find it.

The great mass of humanity has identified happiness with what money can buy, and it struggles desperately to conquer these riches in order to be happy. When people manage to obtain these riches and the advantages they offer, they find they are not happy and begin to think that they were mistaken. Experience teaches that happiness should not be confused with pleasure. True happiness is hidden within the human heart. It is as if a small bird dwells within it, which upon awakening sings to us and produces ineffable joy. When we do not hear its song, surely it is because it is frightened by the "external noise," and that it yearns for our care, while happiness fades away. It is not material pleasures that stimulate its song, but that which dwells within the soul.

Happiness is a purely internal state in which nothing that happens externally, intervenes. To be happy is to have found internal peace, to have found oneself. Unhappiness arises from the division of the "I" of the individual. The individual is constantly changing because he has no single and indivisible "I." When one manages to find a moment of happiness, his "I" changes, and this happiness fades away.

There is no human being more unfortunate than the one who is a prisoner of conflicting feelings, whose heart is completely open to all the emotional vibrations which surround him. This poor person is like a human weather vane which swings to the side dictated by the emotional vibrations which penetrate him. This individual suffers unspeakably as he is constantly oscillating between happiness and misfortune. When he thinks he is stepping at last onto the firm ground of happiness, the ground sinks beneath him and everything fades away. Desperation has reached him, and he will know no peace until his psychic pendulum swings the other way.

The only path towards happiness is through educating the heart to feel, by leading it to feel only when guided by reason. In this way, the door is closed to negative psychic vibrations.

The greatest happiness reigns when the heart is at peace. It is not a matter of killing one's feelings but rather of training them to be conscious and reasonable. It is a question of introducing into the heart, the capacity for reason, without losing the freshness and spontaneity of one's feelings.

The one who educates his heart in this way does not become insensitive but on the contrary, feels more deeply than before, but with consciousness and reason.

There are two great enemies of happiness: pride and egoism. The conceited individual will never be happy except when he undergoes the ordeal of consciously humbling himself until his humiliation no longer causes him suffering, at which point he can refrain from humility for he has conquered himself.

All proud people suffer from an inferiority complex which drives them to assert their personality, adopting attitudes of superiority. In extreme cases their pride drives them to declare war on the rest of humanity. This could be called a "king complex" or "queen complex."

The "king" by decree is constantly endeavoring to show others that he is "something special," that he is different, original and superior. As a child he felt that he was inferior to others, for real or imagined reasons. Among the imaginary reasons for this complex, could be a lack of family love, especially the love of his parents. Because this child could not stand feeling inferior, he gave himself over to the imaginary creation of himself as a superior being full of ideal qualities. This being lives in his subconscious and can be called the "idealized image." Since he is never able to live up to his "idealized image," he reacts as a proud, dominant and deeply sarcastic personality. Deep inside himself he desires to humiliate others because he feels humiliated himself upon realizing that he is not recognized nor treated as a king or the superman of his "idealized image." He is very unhappy if he cannot demonstrate his superiority, and due to this, he may react by trying to become a great success, either commercially, artistically or in any other way, which would place him in a privileged position with respect to the rest of the world. Since he is not recognized in the way his "idealized image" warrants, he takes revenge through his pride which he uses as a shield and weapon to enforce his "powerful personality."

He is by nature profoundly distrustful and believes everyone is cheating him. This feeling originates within himself and is a subterfuge to present to the world that which is not real, a false personality. He is also obstinate and twisted because he considers compromising and lending a hand, a humiliation.

The remedy lies in the decision to undergo the "terrible humiliation" of being just one more human being, without any more special rights or privileges than the rest of humanity.

This "idealized image," which we all create to a certain extent, may induce us to lose sight of our true happiness by leading us to pursue objectives that we really do not desire, other than to make us feel superior.

We must learn to be happy with what we have and not to live continually awaiting some special gift which we believe will make us happy. One who is not happy with what he has will never reach true happiness. It is necessary to live in the present; the only reality is *now*; the past and future are never real. Being able to awaken each morning in one's own bed, being able to breathe, to see what happens in each moment, to hear the song of birds, enjoy breakfast, and fully live each small moment; these are the realities.

We must live each moment of our life as if it were the last.

How different life would be, for example, if we knew we were going to die in 24 hours. We would live fully, and never would the air be more precious, nor the light so essential.

There are two magic words whose truth enfolds the master keys to happiness: *to love and to give.*

One who does not love cannot be happy. This is

what Jesus meant when he said, *"love one another."*

If mothers started to teach love and tolerance to their children now, the world would change, because people would change internally. What is it that drives men to mutual destruction, to bloody wars, tyranny, political assassination and all the terrible ills of humanity, if not a lack of consciousness? The predominance of the bestial part in man over his intelligence?

Together with receiving a body that belongs to the animal kingdom, man also receives the terrible inheritance of bestiality. The animal, which fights only for its own survival, has no concern about the destruction of its own species if it can save itself. This is the curse of humanity: its bestiality. We are gods in the bodies of beasts and the entire world is in the hands of the "great beast," that is, man himself. Whoever surrenders to the beast within, obtains honors, triumphs and riches but at the cost of the loss of his own will and consciousness.

It is for this reason that life has always been hard and difficult for those chosen spirits within whom reign love and consciousness.

We all know the reaction of the "great beast" when the one called Jesus Christ preached love and brotherhood among men. This *Savior* was crucified by the "beast" who saw that his kingdom was seriously threatened, but Christ bequeathed us his message of love and fraternity. This is the reason why there are so many lies and so much deceit in the world. Anyone who speaks the truth provokes the anger of the beast and suffers something similar to a crucifixion.

The only path to the evolution and salvation of the human race is by the domination of its bestiality through the spirit or divine part. This is the true regeneration hidden behind the symbolic "I.N.R.I." that was written over the head of Christ.

There are innumerable stumbling blocks in the path for those who wish to wear the crown of consciousness, because the beast is expert in the art of masquerade, since if this were not so, it would be readily recognized. It generally adopts the disguise of love and goodness for gathering disciples and then uses them as instruments.

Why, for example, is the image of Jesus Christ nailed to the cross maintained, as if it were necessary to celebrate, remember and perpetuate this event?

Human evolution has followed a totally unilateral course, because on the one hand, there have been great scientific advances, but on the other, man has not conquered himself and is in the same situation as a group of six year old children playing with guns, atomic bombs and missiles. What is the use of so much material progress if we are not capable of making conscious use of these powers? We are not even able to act consciously with our own physical bodies, yet we want to land on the moon and conquer the Cosmos.

Occultism, or the wise use of the forces of Nature which influence the life of man, is the only path we can take to reach an integral transformation of the human race through the development of consciousness. The highest ideal of this science is to attain world peace under one government, doing away with borders between countries, so that only one people will exist: the Earth.

For this to come to pass, Christ would have to return to earth, in the form of a new Messiah who would again fight to enchain the beast.

If triumphant, a new period of spiritual splendor could begin for all humanity, and the day would dawn when the "I" or spirit would reign over the beast.

Anyone who wants to cooperate with the goal for world peace, should recite daily the following prayer:

> *"In the name of my immortal spirit I ask for peace on earth,*
> *That love and fraternity reign in the heart of all men.*
> *That CHRIST should have the power and strength to overcome evil.*
> *That the LIGHT of the SPIRIT triumph over the darkness of ignorance.*
> *That now and always there should be peace and love on Earth."*

If a great number of people were to say this prayer daily, concentrating all their faith on its fulfillment, they would fill the planet with vibrations of love and peace which would powerfully influence the maintaining of world peace.

Let us not forget the basic principle that *"Everything is Mind; the Universe is mental."* From the moment we realize that *everything is Mind* and that happiness and misfortune are only opposite poles of the same thing, we will be able to use our mental power *to transmute* a state of misfortune into one of happiness. Furthermore, for this transmutation to be lasting, we must learn to isolate ourselves from the low and undesirable vibrations which surround the soul of the planet and which are those born of base instincts and human passions.

One who wishes to keep pure and clean, and avoid these lower vibrations is in a similar situation to that of a man who is dressed in white who has to cross a muddy swamp. Low or evil vibrations are transmitted just like the germs of a plague.

A woman who has just fought with her husband and who then visits a friend carries with her the vibrations of strife, anger and annoyance, leaving these vibrations in the house, as well as in the double etheric of her friend, who will suffer some disturbance as a result.

The only way to shield oneself from these

negative vibrations is to attain complete psychic mastery in order not to be caught by them.

Psychic mastery is fundamental to the search for happiness, and the heart, is equivalent to the tuning knob of our internal receiver. If we tune in to a low vibration, we take on all the forces in that vibratory field and it will become difficult for us to withdraw from these negative states.

Everything we have discussed up to now refers to the happiness of the "I," which is the only true, lasting and real happiness. Bodily happiness is reached by satisfying the purely physical needs of the mass, such as eating, drinking, procreating, owning beautiful clothes and expensive cars so that everyone we meet can see how successful we are. It is odd how the human being identifies himself with the needs of his body, to the extreme of being unable to distinguish reality from illusion. The body constantly demands many things: food, pleasure, comfort and especially the company of other masses. This is clearly seen in the case of love, because it is possible for one who knows these laws to distinguish immediately between love and mere physical attraction.

A couple might swear eternal love over and over, and feel as if their hearts might break when they are apart, being completely convinced that they love as nobody ever loved before, as nobody could ever love, while true love may be entirely absent from their relationship.

The mass of this woman needs the mass of that man because by uniting, they duplicate their energy-mass which of course brings about physical satisfaction. One of the characteristics of this pseudo-love is that the woman does not surrender wholeheartedly to the man if he does not first surrender himself totally and completely to her.

Therefore, the woman's physical being wishes then to possess the man's physical being entirely and she thus loses her femininity upon taking the active or masculine role, that is the role of the male.

This is the surest sign for recognizing if true love exists between a man and a woman. The woman who really loves, surrenders herself without demanding anything; she gives without seeking anything in exchange, in the same way as Nature offers all its gifts to man without expecting anything in return. This woman thinks only of the happiness of her partner and not how he can make her happy.

A man who really loves a woman will remain at her side, giving all his support, even if she is only seeking her own comfort and advantage.

Happiness in love is perhaps the most difficult to obtain, since the existence of true love, and for that true love to be reciprocated, is almost impossible to achieve. Generally, true love is unilateral, and is not reciprocated in the same measure.

Those who wish to find happiness in love should be attentive to the following advice so that their natures are in complete harmony. Neither a man nor a woman is one hundred percent one sex, because each person carries a certain amount of the energy of the opposite sex.

A man, for example, may be 80% male and 20% female.

This part of the opposite sex within a human being provokes all the disharmony in marriage for when this part surfaces, there is an immediate clash of vibrations of the same polarity and repulsion is inevitable, because it is well known that like poles repel and opposite poles attract.

A woman should dispassionately analyze herself to discover which of her attitudes are feminine and which are masculine. She must never try to dominate the man or to be possessive, as these attitudes automatically close the door to success. She must be careful that her words do not injure the psyche of her partner with negative and destructive suggestions. It is quite common to hear an angry wife say to her husband: "You are useless and good for nothing." If she knew the enormous damage she was causing with her harsh words, she would carefully avoid them. Together with becoming slowly but surely what she insinuates, a man will feel a strong resentment towards her because he feels that his masculine dignity, pride and virility have been questioned and that he is being treated as a naughty child.

This is the most sure way for a woman to lose her man. She should never try to impose her will imperiously. If she wishes to obtain something it must be with sweetness, love and subtle suggestion, so that he feels he is giving and not being obliged to do so. The woman who knows how to reign supreme in the heart of a man will obtain everything from him without even asking. A man needs a woman beside him who will boost his virility and manliness, not one who undermines him. Happy is the one who is loved and respected by his wife.

Is it not better for a wife to obtain everything from her husband by respecting and being in harmony with him instead of making his life difficult so that he surrenders in the end in order to live in peace?

I can assure all dominant women that their husbands do not really love them and that they live with them only out of habit and fear.

A dominant woman will never be able to keep her man, because as she has positive or masculine vibrations, she will never be able to satisfy him sexually.

When a woman is profoundly feminine and surrenders her soul and spirit to her man, she will always be the only one, and there will be no woman, no matter how beautiful, who will be capable of taking him from her side.

Let us explore more deeply the psychology of the dominant woman as this point is important both to men and to women, because the dominant woman or "Diana" can only be happy with a man who has an Oedipus Complex and who is most happy to have a mother who dominates him.

Contrary to what is supposed, the Oedipus Complex and the Electra Complex are quite common. Nevertheless, they pass unobserved because usually these complexes develop at an early age and are deeply embedded in the subconscious and provoke certain reactions which are rarely attributed to these complexes.

The woman who does not overcome the Electra Complex and eradicate this obsession from her mind, will never be able to fulfill herself sexually and emotionally.

She feels an instinctive hate for men because she thinks she is being cheated, despised and hurt by her progenitor because he does not fulfill her desire to be joined to him.

Many times, she turns into a "devourer of men" with the wish to destroy them as a means of destroying both the hated and beloved images of her father which have been engraved on her subconscious.

With each man whom she unites with, this terrible duality within her manifests which can easily lead to misfortune. On the one hand she loves her partner, but as soon as the image of her father surfaces, she hates him because she identifies him with her progenitor and thus feels humiliated and despised, just as she felt deceived and disdained by her father in her childhood when she saw him with "another woman."

The moment arises when this woman says, "love does not exist for me." Therefore, it can never exist because she unconsciously seeks "the father's image" in other men, but when she finds it, the terrible struggle between love and hate, attraction and repulsion begins again.

The best thing that could happen to her would be to fall deeply in love with a man of high moral and spiritual qualities and surrender to him totally and completely. If this should happen, it is possible that the image of this man could erase the father's image, and she could attain the long awaited happiness.

In what could be called a simulation of love, the dominant woman unconsciously forces the man to adopt a false personality entirely in keeping with what she alone desires, repressing at the same time, all that displeases her. Everything he does is to please her, to make her happy and to avoid unpleasantness because he fears her tantrums and bad temper.

This confirms her masculine character because

she has possessed her man by forcing him to adapt to her personality. Can it be said that she loves him? Naturally not, since she has created a toy for herself, limited to giving her pleasure because it acts exactly as she wishes. This is anti-Nature and is artificial, and we must not forget that all that is anti-Nature is punished because it goes against Nature. The punishment received by the man who acts in this role, is the lack of that power given to him by Nature. He will struggle fruitlessly and will not be able to attain success unless he finds another, more feminine woman. The more feminine his woman, the more giving power he will have, because he finds in her all the gifts of Mother Nature.

I do not wish all this to be interpreted in the sense that woman should be a slave to man. It is only that she should at all times maintain her real role as a woman.

Woman represents for man the earthly manifestation of the feminine part of God. She symbolizes for him, purity, love, sweetness and inspiration. Because she intimately represents an ideal, man suffers a tremendous psychological shock when she adopts vulgar, brutal or masculine attitudes. This shock may be sufficient to kill all his love.

A woman should always be sweet, gentle, spiritually delicate, loving, attentive and understanding, surrendering to him without reservation, respecting him in all ways. Her love for him should be the balm which dissipates the disappointments of life and which transforms them into happiness.

She is a fairy with a magic wand who has the power to plunge the man into despair or give him total and complete happiness. With her magic wand she can ward off evil, allowing only goodness to reign.

Unfortunately for humanity, there are women who do not use this power to protect their men, but instead use it to unload evil upon them and to finally destroy them.

The man for his part must strengthen all his masculine and virile qualities in order to take his companion firmly by the hand along the path of life.

Subconsciously, a woman wants her partner to possess her entirely in every sense of the word, not just sexually. He should possess her personality, her soul, her heart and her spirit.

On one side, he should be very loving toward her, and on the other, firm and severe, in order not to lose his masculine condition.

His strength should be that which guides her beauty.

She should be able to fully feel his masculine and virile strength.

In love as in everything else, the law of action and reaction is inexorably fulfilled, and one receives the same as one irradiates to one's partner. Therefore, if a woman for instance, constantly nags and treats her partner badly, he will be driven by this negative force to commit actions which will make her suffer.

All women who wish to keep their partners should remember that chains of flowers are stronger than chains of iron.

Man for his part should always remember that woman is by nature much more sensitive, delicate and psychic than he, and he should therefore treat her at all times with sweet firmness and severe gentleness. At all times he must be ready to give her his complete support, both materially and spiritually. If there is one thing that disillusions a woman, it is that her partner should lose the kindness and romanticism in their amorous relationship. She needs him to tell her frequently that he loves her and not to limit himself to using her sexually to satisfy his instincts.

The golden law for a man to keep his wife's love is as follows: "Always treat your wife as if she were your sweetheart, as if you had recently met and were declaring your love. Look at her as if it were the first time, when you fell in love with her." The one who is clever enough to apply these principles wisely, will have a married life which will be an eternal honeymoon. The saddest thing is when a couple gets so used to each other that they stay together out of habit rather than love.

A curious thing happens in most marriages. At the beginning the couple is desperately in love, but gradually their love fades and disappears, and if they do not separate, they fall into a life held together only by routine. Their love, which should strengthen as the years go by, disappears instead.

This leads us to a sad and inevitable conclusion. Love which disappears as time goes by, until it degenerates into habit, is not love. This type of union is only the result of passion. Once passion has been satisfied, a vacuum remains. Each blames the other, but neither accepts the reality that a love which was never there, cannot disappear.

The passionate union is characterized by repeated break ups and make ups during married life. After a period of loving, a sudden fight occurs and with it, a period of something resembling hate. Then love returns and the cycle is indefinitely repeated.

True love is characterized by the fact that it increases with time and does not diminish as the years go by. Although there are occasional fights, they never produce a psychological separation, nor create barriers, and on the contrary, the couple's love increases.

Each partner seeks the happiness of the other rather than his own. It is incredible how small details influence married life. The woman, for example, must never lose her modesty nor present herself to her man in an unkempt manner. The hermetic principle of "as it is above, so it is below and as it is below, so it is above" is clear in this case. If the couple were to sit down to dinner, he unshaven and she without makeup, with hair uncombed, or otherwise untidy, this same disorder will also reflect on their mutual relationship, which will be of a low spiritual vibration.

An extremely happy marriage would be one where each endeavors to make life happier for the other, with pleasant surprises or small gifts.

The husband, for example, should be romantic and bring flowers to his wife, show interest in her problems and be ready to demonstrate his love. He must be husband, lover, friend, father and brother. If he fails in any of these, he will not make his wife happy. She should also care for him and make his home life pleasant. With a little feminine intelligence, she will know how to make his home a true paradise.

If she is able to make his home an oasis of calm, tranquility and happiness, he will long for the moment when he comes home, to have his wife at his side.

She also must assume the role of wife, lover, mother, friend and sister.

Perhaps for those who are not sufficiently mature, or for the passionate, egotistical, fanatical or obtuse, or for all who have not a speck of insight, everything presented in this book will be words and only words. However, the one who knows what humanity is, who knows what love is, and who has perceived the existence of a supreme being, will see the light. Not all are capable of seeing the light. Can one explain to a man born blind what light is? To the deaf, what music is?

Since we are speaking of happiness and love we must deal with the materialization of the active and passive principles, that is, children.

No couple has the right to bring a child into the world if they have not at least some certainty of producing a healthy child, without physical or psychological defects and with a background that will permit it to obtain success.

For this, there are immutable laws which control the "quality" of the being who is brought into the world. These laws are as follows:

1. At the moment of conception, there should exist a complete psychic, amorous and instinctive harmony between husband and wife. The more positive and sublime their state of mind just before intercourse, the more sublime will be the conception, and a superior child will be formed.

2 . Once the woman is pregnant, *she must not be touched by the man until after birth.* All sexual relations during pregnancy cause irreparable damage to the nervous system of the unborn child.

3. During pregnancy, the wife should be surrounded by all types of comforts and no worries. She should be surrounded by beautiful things, listen to good music and endeavor to keep calm and serene at all times, so that she can transmit all these positive vibrations to the child she is carrying.

Once the baby is born, she must ensure that the child leads a healthy life, in contact with the elements. The child must realize from the beginning that his parents are in charge, because all babies instinctively try to dominate their parents, first by crying, and afterwards with temper tantrums.

Firmness and love should be perfectly balanced, because when one or the other is lacking, serious complexes arise. The modern custom is to give children all they ask for at the cost of great sacrifice, just for them to have better toys and better clothing so they are not "ashamed to face their playmates."

Familial relations within the home should be perfectly controlled and directed. It is terrible for a child to witness fights between his parents because, for him, they are really like gods.

Before the age of seven, it is difficult to make a child understand with kind words and reasoning, because he has not yet developed the first sparkle of consciousness, which occurs when he is about eight years old.

A firm, but loving attitude on the part of parents is desirable, and in certain cases physical punishment can be used, but only when intelligently applied and controlled.

When a mother or a father reach a point where their child makes them lose their temper, it is because the child is subtly, but surely dominating them. Can a father help a child over whom he has no power? Can a mother help her children if she cannot maintain her calm?

During childhood, when the second creation, or second birth begins, which is as important as the first, it is then that the parents should make the maximum effort to transmit to their children the best of themselves. Children are extremely observant and they never forget what has impressed them in one way or another. A father who leaves one day forgetting to kiss his small daughter may create in her a sensation of abandonment, because that particular day she may just have been in a hyper-sensitive psychic state.

A child who finds in his mother callousness, selfishness and a lack of sensitivity will grow up with an immense sense of loneliness.

Parents should always remember that children expect the best from them, that which is the most sublime. They must try to keep a balance, exerting neither too much nor too little sensitivity.

Along with the onset of puberty, the number one problem of sex appears. The greatest error parents can make is to avoid giving sexual instruction to their children, because with this attitude, they leave their children free to their own initiatives and discoveries. The mother should explain the subject to her daughter in a delicate but natural way, as if they were speaking about the pollination of flowers. The father should give every kind of information to his sons when he considers the appropriate time has come.

There is nothing more beautiful than a father who becomes a friend to his children, when they have lost their fear of him, but not their respect. It is impossible for a father to understand his children's problems if he does not momentarily put aside his role as a father and become a friend, sharing their points of view.

When the head of the household is able to guide his children and his wife wisely, this familial group becomes a powerful force of life, love and protection for them all, where happiness will certainly reign.

Many readers may perhaps have bitter thoughts with respect to happiness, such as:

How can I be happy if I am sick?
How can I be happy if I suffer economic stress?
How can I be happy if I have such "bad luck?"
And the list of "but's" only compounds these.

For those who think like this, two points must be emphasized: all that we find in life, either good or bad, is the product of what we ourselves have brought about. We reap what we sow.

Everything is vibration, both good or evil.

Every vibration can be changed into its opposite with the power of the mind as everything is Mind and everything vibrates in the Universe.

Hate can be transformed into love, failure into success, poverty into abundance, pain into pleasure and suffering into peace.

All transmutation requires the necessary time to happen and patience, faith and a spirit of sacrifice are the three essential elements of success.

All those who firmly believe that they can change the negative into positive, will be able to do so with their Mind and will power.

The hidden energies of the human being are

extremely powerful. There are times when these powers automatically appear and the individual doubles his strength and intelligence, as for example, when he is in danger of death. "He can who believes he can" is a saying with undoubtable power, as it illustrates that *faith*, as the feminine element, and *active thought*, as the masculine element, are both necessary to bring about *mental creation*.

The one who thinks he has "bad luck" should erase this thought from his psyche forever and should only fill his being with the vibrations of success.

See success, feel success, hear success, smell success, breathe success. Your only thoughts should be of success, success, success.

If you proceed this way you will reach your objective.

Transmutation means to consciously reject the undesirable and affirm the desirable.

Nothing is impossible for the one who uses this principle wisely.

CHAPTER XVIII

THE PATH TO INITIATION

As mentioned in previous pages, the one who is called an Initiate is the one who studies and comes to know the occult laws of life, the way the forces of Nature act upon man.

In ancient times, initiation took place in the temples of Egypt and Greece under the most severe conditions, as an extremely rigorous selection was made so that only those of outstanding moral and spiritual qualities could be really and truly initiated. These temples were veritable fortresses where the one who sought initiation either passed the tests as victors or never came out again, because those who failed remained on in the capacity of servants or slaves.

It was in Egypt where many spiritual supermen received directly from the priests, the science which enabled them to "create themselves" or to *regenerate*, and among these was Jesus himself.

The candidate for initiation arrived without any previous knowledge, armed only with an intense desire to learn the truth, *the knowledge of mysteries or the laws of Nature as symbolized by Isis.*

What were these men being taught?

What was done in those temples to permit the likes of a Pythagoras, for example, to come forth?

In its purest form *the science of sciences* known as *Occultism* was given to these men, and this knowledge has been zealously guarded and transmitted. By means of this knowledge it was possible to transmute the inferior or passionate nature of the student until he was completely identified with his own spirit.

Until this was attained, the neophyte had to overcome innumerable obstacles placed in his path to demonstrate his true spiritual character. Many were those who failed these tests, and very few triumphed.

Those who triumphed went out into the world to fulfill through their work their aims for the benefit of humanity, because the Initiate solemnly promises to employ all knowledge and power received for the good of Humanity.

The Initiate's secret labor is aimed towards world peace and to attain this, he works silently without ever seeking the approval or the applause of the masses.

Through the ages, the great Initiates have been the true guides or teachers of Humanity. Nevertheless, the majority of them have lived in secret and no one has ever been aware of their work. What is the reason for the secrecy and discretion of the Initiates?

They are aware that all action causes reaction and that the "beast" furiously attacks the one who openly initiates a work of true human recuperation.

By recalling the martyrdom of Jesus, the fate of the Great Master, Jacob of Molay who was burned at the stake at the command of Clement V and Phillip the Beautiful, and the tortures during the Inquisition, we can understand why it is necessary to work in silence and secrecy.

Nature confers her wealth to every being without distinction, and because of this, the knowledge of her secrets is justified only in its use for the benefit of all.

In fact today, the door to initiation is open to all; to all persons without distinction of race or creed.

But how many are capable of finding the true doorway?

Thousands of doors beckon, each one bearing the sign: "Entrance to the path of Wisdom and Truth."

Without a doubt, only one of these leads to *true*

initiation and a true knowledge of the mysteries of Nature.

The one who merits passage through this portal will be guided by his immortal spirit. The one who does not merit this, will seek entrance eternally, but will never find it. Jesus said: "Many are called, but few are chosen."

Actually, what is known about initiation is buried under a tangle of falsehood and lies, precisely because Occultism has been categorized as magic and witchcraft. Its true significance has been totally lost, that is, of a knowledge that enables the bestial human to be transformed into a true representative of God on earth.

There are innumerable schools in the world which teach or pretend to teach Occultism, but they are only study groups that do not confer real initiation upon the individual, which is the only thing that can awaken the spiritual flame. One who has no spiritual flame is only a talking machine that repeats what he has read or has been taught. It is necessary to search carefully, requesting that our own spirit lead and guide us to the truth. Before doing so, a deep examination of one's conscience should be made to determine whether one really wishes knowledge of the truth, as truth is only for strong men, not for children. We must ask ourselves if we are willing to abandon our personality and sacrifice ourselves for the good of all. The world is undergoing a crucial period and is in desperate need of just, strong, wholehearted and upright men, imbued with the ideals of peace, love, abundance and good for all mankind.

Where are these men? Where is a Pythagoras now, a Socrates or a Plato, men who illuminated the world by their example? Where is a Leonardo da Vinci, a Raphael or a Michelangelo who cast their creative genius upon all?

It seems as if the light that illuminated the world in other ages has been extinguished. Scientific advances have not been sufficient, as the spirit also needs nourishment. We are passing through a time when the beast walks the world without hindrance, in which moral and spiritual values have fallen. Nevertheless, the light of initiation still burns brightly during these times in various parts of the world, and it is there that we must seek spiritual elevation and it is from there that we can learn to conquer our human passions and replace them with virtues.

Love must reign upon the earth, and to achieve this end, each human being has the inescapable obligation to seek moral and spiritual elevation and thus contribute to world peace.

In the soul of the planet Earth, nothing is ever lost. An evil word, a curse, a state of hate or rage are veritable chains which shackle suffering humanity.

You, who are reading this, what path do you

wish to follow? That of the egoist who uses the earth's soul as a receptacle for garbage, or that of one who gives of his best, his love, his tolerance, his good wishes and his joy of living?

It is necessary to effectively help cultivate the invisible garden of this planet where all our energy is maintained, because as was said before, *nothing is lost.* The soul of the planet Earth is similar to the fertile ground which brings to life all the seeds sown within it; equally, the soul of the planet also brings to life all the states of mind of the human being, which subsequently and strongly influence world destiny. The one who yearns for *world peace* and *love* must contribute with his own love for Humanity.

For those who desire more than this, and who wish to enter through the portals of initiation, the following considerations must be made:

First, it is necessary to clarify that just as there are many paths for acquiring knowledge and bettering oneself to a greater or lesser degree, the same is true in the case of spiritual cultivation.

However, to reach *true initiation* or rather, *to light the spiritual flame*, there exists only one path, and that is, to enter into contact with an authentic spiritual Guide who will lead the aspirant by the hand along the steep and arduous path. This Guide is the pillar of support for the disciple, without whose support he will never successfully overcome the obstacles which are placed in his path, which will arise from his own inferior or bestial nature, and which will try to desperately resist all attempts to be tamed and educated in order to be lead to obey consciousness.

On the other hand, the disciple will come up against opposition from all those who in one way or another are in the service of the beast. These could be friends, relatives, spouses, brothers, sisters or parents, who will try by all means possible to dissuade his resolve.

There will be many times when his faith in his own "I," in his own *spirit*, will be put to the test.

Let us recall what has been said in previous pages about *consciousness* as opposed to being asleep, and we will realize that it is necessary for the student to undergo a series of psychological jolts which will gradually awaken him from his sleep. These jolts act like alarms and are carefully prepared and studied by the master guide. As a result, the disciple needs to have acquired absolute and complete faith and confidence in his teacher, without being deceived by appearances at any moment, because everything that takes place in an initiatic group, is aimed for the benefit of all who participate in it. Before entering one of these groups, pride, vanity, prejudice, selfishness, and the personality or personal interests must be left aside. A conquest as great as contacting one's own spirit is not easily accomplished. The most common mistake of students is that after a time they forget that they have entered the group to learn and they begin to analyze everything from their own point of view until they eventually distort the truth.

The discipline followed within these groups is neither mystical nor dogmatic. The guide teaches what he already knows well, so that the disciples may put into practice what they learn and by their own experience, prove its effectiveness.

It must be established here that the path of Initiation is very arduous and cannot be taken lightly, as it may be dangerous for the student who does not strictly adhere to the teacher's instructions.

To give an idea of this danger, I will say only this: to contact one's own spirit one must first die, in order to be reborn. This symbolic death is the destruction of "personalism," that is, all that is artificial in the individual, his mental "automatisms." These automatisms make up the wall that exists between man and his spirit. This artificial part that was acquired from outside influences is what must be destroyed, so as to be re-created afterwards according to the essence, or spirit. If a disciple withdraws from the group for any reason whatsoever, immediately after this mental automatism is destroyed, he will experience an internal vacuum, without any support and nothing to grasp on to, which may naturally result in many negative consequences. As a result of this, the guide is no longer responsible for the disciple from the moment that he stops obeying him.

Since the first step is to destroy all that is negative, all complexes or vices of the student must be eliminated, until the soul is totally cleansed. Nothing should remain in his subconscious; the teacher should take on the role of a psychiatrist, but a psychiatrist who knows exactly how to destroy the root of the destructive weed which manifests itself in the form of a complex. The disciple should trust in him completely and be totally sincere in his confidences; he must not tell half-truths, because if he deceives his teacher, he will be deceiving himself; for it is the teacher's task to help the disciple realize that all he yearns for is hidden deep within his own soul. If the disciple due to pride, disbelief or distrust refuses to follow the recommendations of his teacher, he is denying himself with his attitude, as he is following the dictates of the beast within himself.

The disciple must never forget that he has two intelligences within himself which represent good and evil, light and darkness, evolution and involution. This dual intelligence consists of the internal master or divine force and the bestial or involutive force, which tries by all means possible to prevent his evolution. Initiation is a long road which gradually leads the aspirant to communication with his own internal master. Until this moment arrives, he must blindly obey his physical teacher who is the visible and tangible representative of his internal master.

As long as he strictly fulfills his Master's instructions, the disciple is safeguarded from the beast.

Man alone cannot overcome his beast, because it is within himself and therefore, he must relinquish his will to his teacher for him to conquer it. All initiation is a struggle between good and evil, between the blind, bestial and destructive force of the disciple and the intelligent consciousness of the guide. Two paths open before him simultaneously: one path where the Teacher says yes, and the other where the beast says no. This is why the disciple must obey the teacher's will as he is the only one who can save him from following the dictates of the beast. When the beast has been completely enchained, then the disciple will recover his will and the Teacher becomes his counselor and instructor. He is no longer one who obliges him to do such and such. This obedience demanded by the teacher is the first barrier that the candidate who is seeking the truth, comes up against, as it is terribly difficult to renounce one's own will and obey that of another. Many crash against this barrier and renounce to go further. If we examine this matter objectively, we will discover that, in reality, the candidate does not sacrifice or renounce his will for the simple reason that he never had one as we established at the beginning of this book when speaking about Man. When he obeys the guide, the student is mentally harmonizing with his own internal master; the guide is repeating to the disciple what his own internal master requires from him.

From this perspective, we can understand that filling the student with theoretical knowledge or participating in ceremonies to exalt his consciousness are only illusory, because until he has conquered the beast, there is no possible evolution or path for him to follow.

Real black magic is giving knowledge of the use of mental power to those who are dominated by the beast, because such knowledge will be used by the beast to satisfy its own instincts and drag others with it into the abyss.

For this reason, a Master is very careful not to bestow knowledge which may be dangerous, upon those who have not been able to shed their own bestiality. During his work with a disciple, the teacher subjects him to repeated tests to verify his advancement. These tests are such that the disciple does not realize he is undergoing them, and it is necessary for it to be this way because an attempt is being made to obtain totally authentic reactions from the disciple, precisely to see if he is really attaining self domination.

From this point of view, the teacher has the dual role of "good angel" and "angel of temptation," because on one hand, he conveys his wisdom to his disciple and counsels him at all times, while on the other, he subjects him to harsh tests and temptations to strengthen him in order to be able to gauge his true spiritual character.

We could call man an intelligent animal and his animal part possesses an extraordinary intelligence which is dedicated solely to its own goals of involution or animalization of the divine part or consciousness; that is, as an animal, he wishes to drag the spirit down to his own level, to the point of completely absorbing it within himself. Since the beast is aware of the weaknesses of the individual, it attacks his most vulnerable aspects to dissuade him from initiation. It insinuates, for example, that an individual with the candidate's intelligence and will should not obey another individual who is a man just like himself, as this would be slavery. It causes him to doubt, fear and distrust the Master's teachings. It puts in his path, obstacles that would be insurmountable for those who are not determined at all costs to reach their goals. It is for this reason that few can achieve anything concrete and tangible on the Initiate's path, since the beast tenaciously refuses to be dominated by the will of the disciple. When the individual has advanced in such a way that the beast sees his dominion in danger, it offers him those material things he has longed for all his life.

Will he be steadfast in his determination to develop spiritually if he falls in love for example, with a woman who only gives her love on the condition that he abandon the occult path, or if fortune favors him and he attains great wealth?

In the most subtle ways, obstacles will be placed before him that can imperceptibly turn him from his path, and it is then that the authenticity of his desire for spiritual evolution will be proven, for his original motivation may have been purely materialistic or emotional. A man may wish to renounce everything and follow such a path because he feels there is nothing for him in life and that fortune has denied him what others have received. If he undertakes the path of Initiation and then later finds these gifts of which he has been deprived, all his interests for spiritual elevation will suddenly cease, because his "spiritual" craving was only a pretext for attaining his own personal desires. It must be repeated that Initiation is a path of renunciation and sacrifice and the use of the power that comes from dominion of the forces of Nature, is not justifiable if that power is not used exclusively for the benefit of Humanity.

Another error the student frequently commits is to try to judge the actions of his Master in the light of his own mentality. This is truly impossible because the Master exists at a level of consciousness that is much higher than that of the student's who thus cannot elevate himself to see that which the Master observes.

Consequently, it is also an error to analyze "reasonably" the advice received from the Master in order to decide later whether or not to follow it, as there can be no half measures: either one obeys completely in everything or one does not obey at all. Before reaching this state of obedience, which is the only state that enables the aspirant true and effective spiritual fulfillment, there are other degrees of contact with the Master, which are only recommended, but not obligatory. These degrees of contact are only preparation for the true alchemical transmutation which the Master affects upon the student. The Master is extremely demanding with those who aspire to be disciples and he tests them for a long time before definitively accepting them as disciples. This requirement is understandable when one becomes aware that when a teacher receives a new disciple, he automatically burdens himself with all the disciple's karma and becomes directly responsible for his actions. If the disciple subsequently fails or defrauds the Master, the Master will have unnecessarily burdened himself with a large amount of karma from which he will have to gradually free himself by means of the spiritual transmutation of his internal being.

Some set out on the path of initiation solely because of their desire to satisfy their intellectual curiosity. They take this lightly, thinking that it means only the studying of natural laws, but not realizing that they have undertaken a struggle toward consciousness which will surely bring about a complete change in their lives. When students see the reactions provoked by the path they have undertaken in their desire for greater consciousness, they become fearful and withdraw to their previous life of unconsciousness in which they will see nothing because they walk blindfolded.

One who desires to be initiated must thirst for the truth and convert his spiritual path into the most important and most essential prime objective of his life. It is a waste of time to take this as something secondary for a few hours a week and then to forget it. Spiritual discipline is something that must be present at all times because it is a transformation within the soul of the individual and, therefore, is something inseparable from his very being.

Is there anyone who has understood the real scope of Initiation?

It is the *greatest prize* man can win as it is the return to Paradise where there is no ugliness or pain. It is the path which leads to heaven, a true stairway to God, that is, *to the superconscious spiritual part of the mind principle.*

What can be more desirable than Initiation? Honor, riches, love?

These are only illusory states which fade away with the passing of time. The only really lasting and immortal thing is that which is within one's own soul. All else cannot be taken onto the plane of energy when our physical life ceases to exist. All that is material is fleeting and changeable and therefore illusory. All that is spiritual is eternal and immortal.

We envy children because they live completely in a world apart from adults, a world of innocence, purity and happiness, as if they were constantly in contact with *God*. Thus, Initiation is the return to the original purity of man, a return to innocence, to the womb, but this time, the return to Mother Nature herself.

The true Initiate is innocent and pure as a child, but at the same time, wise and intelligent so that it is impossible to take advantage of his innocence. He must be gentle as a dove and sly as a fox. Let us recall the words of Jesus: "Let little children come unto me." The hidden meaning behind what has just been stated should be translated and interpreted thusly: "Let the initiated come unto me." Jesus always spoke in parables, because he knew the truth would burn and destroy those not ready to receive it. He also knew that to speak the truth was and is dangerous. The world does not like truth; it prefers pleasant lies to the naked truth. Anyone who has ever felt that there is something wrong with his life, that there is something disastrous or fatal in the life of man, or an absolute impotency to control fate and to live the life one intimately desires, will realize that man is not perfect, that he is controlled by certain unknown influences from the time of birth until his death. It is as if after a lifetime of work and sacrifice, a great hand appears and suddenly wrests from him the fruits of his efforts, leaving him as naked as when he entered into the world, ready to start another life of sacrifice and new experiences.

Initiation is freedom, freedom from that mysterious influence which controls man as if he were a puppet.

Nevertheless, there are those who think that Initiation consists of sitting, praying and meditating for an hour a day. This is the path of the indolent, who have a small amount of desire to evolve spiritually, but who are too lazy to do anything concrete towards their moral and spiritual development. Initiation is activity, lots of activity. It implies a tenacious and bloody fight; it is sacrifice and more sacrifice, because self dominion is something that is not reached in a year, or even two. It means to oblige the body to totally surrender to the last cell to the will of the spirit for being used consciously. This does not mean that it is necessary to weaken and subject the body to terrible privations as do the Hindus. On the contrary, it is necessary to have the physical body as strong and healthy as possible and this is only attained by forcing it to super-activity, which activates forces not usually used, because the body which is accustomed to sleeping seven to eight hours, eating large quantities and doing as it pleases, does not need them.

I repeat, internal transformation is attained by and through external or physical actions. Each constructive action undertaken physically causes a change in the psyche of the individual. Each physical movement, produces a movement of certain forces on the energetic plane or invisible world. With this key, we lift a corner of the veil that hides liturgical mysteries and the power of signs, symbols and the human word.

Therefore, one who wishes to be initiated must learn to work with his hands, in order to make them conscious and intelligent so that he can transform his own self by means of his works.

All that is learned consciously, becomes a source of energy in the consciousness of the individual which grows and becomes vitalized by activity. On the stairway to consciousness, each one ascends to the step he is capable of reaching, so that the term "consciousness," is also relative because the one who is on the second step is not conscious of the one who is on the third, but he is conscious of the one who is on the first step. Among Initiates, we therefore find different degrees of development, all related to the conquest of qualities which the individual imagines he has but in reality does not have, such as free will and will power for example.

There are many initiates in the world but very few Masters and even fewer Adepts. Much has been speculated regarding the teachers who have been given a supernatural and mysterious character. It is imagined that they live in a continuous state of "unfolding" and that they possess magical powers to dominate Nature and accomplish all they desire. It is believed that they live in inaccessible retreats in India or in the mountains of Tibet. The reality is always more simple and less adorned than fantasy. The fact that a man has attained the degree of Master does not mean that he can avoid his obligations as a citizen or member of society. On the contrary, if a Master wishes to change man and raise his level of consciousness, he must live very close to him so that he is able to carry out his work in his secret way. Social or economic positions mean nothing to such people, as they are conditioned for the work they must accomplish. A

Master may live as a beggar, as a doctor, or a wealthy businessman.   His exterior aspects are of no importance.   He may be physically beautiful or extremely ugly, but the internal radiation is the same in all of them because it is the radiation of *Christ*.

In the presence of a Master an individual feels strangely tranquil and calm, his internal thirst is quenched and he feels the warmth of the radiant magnetism of love, life and the light which emanates from his aura.   One can immediately sense that he is not like other men, but that he is a completely different being.   It is never noticed that these men live in another world as their consciousness dwells on the mental plane.   They may converse with us, be sad or happy, but they are always living on another plane and therefore seem slightly distant and inaccessible.

To be able to instruct, a Master must descend to the plane of his disciples, as the latter cannot ascend to his spiritual level.   If the disciples do not advance along the path, a teacher will be forced to live constantly on a plane lower than his own consciousness, which may make him lose a portion of his spiritual conquests as he tries to raise others to his own sphere.   If on the other hand, his disciples triumph in their undertakings, the teacher can fully use his faculties which will not be damaged by this association with the lower vibrations of others.   Because of this, it is an unwritten law that no disciple has the right to request knowledge which he has neither earned, nor deserved.

The majority of disciples get only a faint idea of the Master's teachings no matter how close they are to him because they are not capable of "wresting" from him the science he has absorbed.

We mentioned before that the conquest of the forces of Nature is justified only for the collective benefit, and therefore all teachers strive to accomplish work for universal benefit.

Therefore, a Master will only teach and enlighten his disciples as much as they cooperate in his work. There is a balance in everything and a teacher cannot make a gift of his knowledge because he is not authorized to do so. All new knowledge, each ray of light, must be earned by the disciple through his own tenacious struggle. Do we not have to fight to feed ourselves? Why then should we expect a guide to feed us spiritually and give us tranquility and comfort at no cost whatsoever? This is the key that will lead us to recognize a true Master. He never makes a gift of light; nothing can be taken from the universal deposit of the *All* without giving something in return, as this would be theft. A true teacher requests something in exchange for his help; he always asks for sacrifices, and the more he asks, the more honored the disciple should feel, because this means that his teacher is disposed to give more to him. The universal balance cannot be altered, and to keep this balance, it is necessary to give, in order to receive. If something is taken from one side of the scale, an equivalent weight must be placed onto the other. Therefore, the occult path is not for the indulgent and lazy, nor for those who prefer only intellectual work and are afraid to dirty their hands with manual labor.

What is explained here is always a source of discord in initiatic groups, as some feel unjustly held back and abandoned, not realizing that the teacher offers his knowledge to those who deserve to receive it. If a disciple should merit credit for his work, his Master will be only too ready to grant it.

From this point of view, the vain words of the pseudo-occultists who say, "occult knowledge cannot be bought," are cause for laughter.

I openly contradict them and say: "Occult knowledge is bought, and at a great price," but not with money. There is no money in the world which can buy the *light*. It can only be bought with sacrifice, dedication, helping others and aiding the Master in his work, regardless of the support received from him.

Everything has its price because this is the law of life, the supreme secret of universal balance. Nothing is received without payment. *"Give and you will receive."*

The power vested in the Teacher or Adept is not his own, but comes from the universal power of All, and as such, it can neither be wasted nor given unless something is received in exchange.

I have hoped to establish this clearly in order to warn those who think that belonging to an initiatic group directed by a Master, means to encounter a fountain of wisdom and spiritual help, without giving anything in return. Everyone who enters an initiatic group, must swear an oath of secrecy, because the knowledge they will receive is solely for them. If a candidate subsequently leaves the group and breaks this oath, he will run the risk of receiving Nature's punishment for violation of a promise he made to his own spirit.

The spiritual state the disciple experiences while following this path is so different, so sublime, that once he has gone beyond a certain limit, he will not be the same being as before, even if he leaves the path entirely. *The occult path is the true nectar of the gods. One who has tasted it, is eternally bound to it and can never again be entirely dominated by the beast.*

In the process of scaling the heights of the gradual awakening of consciousness, a person becomes aware of truths he has never before perceived; he experiences the radiation of the *Universal Mind*, the music of the spheres and the consciousness which even dwells in inanimate matter.

The world where a true Adept resides is so far away and so different that we cannot judge this world according to human canons. He is governed by other laws, other truths, other scales of value. He lives beyond good and evil, beyond pleasure and pain, beyond life and death, as he is with God.

For us, the Adept will be an eternal enigma until we reach his level and we must endeavor to understand him as far as our consciousness permits us to.

This difference between his level and ours, impresses us as a living and inscrutable mystery and when we try to grasp it, it escapes us and gives us the same sensation of unreality that surrounds characters in a fairy tale. During his teachings there are moments when we are not sure whether he is real or unreal, if he exists or not, because he does not have what we could call a particular personality, because he is not fixed in one state of mind, since he is the master of his own feelings.

With respect to the supposedly magical powers of the Adepts, it is interesting to note that they do indeed acquire certain powers, but which are not in any way magical or miraculous. These powers arise from a profound knowledge of the laws of Nature.

Is it possible to have a greater power than the practice of the highest virtues? Can there exist more sublime power than that of an individual who becomes the complete master of his soul?

One who achieves self-mastery transforms and sublimates his animal nature, in order to give birth to his superior "I." When he has really crowned his superior "I" as king of the microcosm which is the body, he undoubtedly has the power to accomplish certain things which are beyond the scope of one who is not the master of his soul.

Nevertheless, the power of powers is the power of love. Yet, who is aware of and truly knows, a true and genuine love?

Who is able to love his enemy? To have a love of simple things, love for animals and even inanimate things?

The Adept is a master of the art of transmutation of vibrations, an alchemist in the complete sense of the word, and possesses the power which all may acquire, to control the smallest vibratory wave within himself. Another characteristic which allows a true Master to be recognized is the double current of force which surrounds him and which is attractive from one side and repulsive from the other.

One who truly wishes for spiritual excellence is drawn to the side of a teacher as if attracted by a magnet. One who has doubts and is only seeking material or purely personal objectives is always faced with invisible opposition which keeps him from establishing contact with the teacher. The Master is always protected and only those who are deserving may reach him.

With everything that has been said in these

pages, we have established that Initiation *is the rebirth of man, a complete regeneration through the vehicle of consciousness. This regeneration permits him to return to his original state of purity, for he comes into contact with his immortal spirit which is the part of God that dwells within him. It is freedom from fate, chance, error, ignorance, vanity and pain; it is to contemplate face to face the truth, and become identified with the universal consciousness or God.*

One who has accomplished this and is fully conscious of his human duties, starts a crusade of impersonal help to Humanity, with the goal of cooperation toward universal peace and to give others an opportunity to acquire the same knowledge he has received. In this way, *a great universal chain of Initiates is formed,* whose origin is lost in antiquity, and whose existence will never end because divine power is infinite and eternal.

If anyone, impelled by a strong desire to learn the truth and attain spiritual superiority in order to help others, wishes to enter the path of Initiation, *I wish to say that the door is open to everyone without distinction of race, creed or class.*

Nevertheless, a dispassionate analysis must be made to determine whether one is willing to give up his personal life for an ideal of peace and universal love.

If not, it is preferable that one's studies be limited to a theoretical knowledge of Occultism, which may be of some use.

One who decides to accept Initiation must seek the only entrance to this path and must seek it within himself, because once this petition to reach a teacher is heard by his spirit, his spirit will lead him safely to a true and authentic Master.

ABOUT THE AUTHOR

John Baines, (literary pseudonym of Dario Salas Sommer), is the contemporary philosopher, founder and director of the Institute for Hermetic Philosophy in Santiago, Chile, with branches worldwide, including the Dario Salas Institute for Hermetic Science in New York City, U.S.A. He has designated his philosophy as a study in the Hermetic Sciences, here defined as "the wise use of Nature's Laws," of principles that date back to Hermes Trismegistus, but as conveyed by Mr. Baines, they are fresh and modern. As a man he encompasses the universal qualities of true humanness by actively promoting the individual development of men and women. His unique perspective, common to all his books, in particular to *The Secret Science, The Stellar Man, The Science of Love, HypsoConsciousness,* and *Morals for the 21st Century,* unites contemporary psychological practice with ancient philosophical wisdom. All his works are intended to enrich and harmonize man's understanding of himself and his relation to all.

Mr. Baines wrote *The Secret Science,* now in its fourth edition, so that the neophyte could visualize the path towards truth and knowledge of Nature's hidden secrets and thus be capable of transcending himself, of raising himself over his animal instincts and of activating and manifesting the higher intelligence of true human beings. The body of this knowledge constitutes the essence of the wisdom of the spiritual supermen of the past.

To The Reader

This letter is intended for the reader who is driven by a spiritual inquietude to deepen his personal knowledge of Hermetic Philosophy on a practical and tangible level. For direct contact with our Headquarters or with any of our other Branches, and for more information regarding talks and instructional meetings held in New York City, I ask you to please write to:

The Dario Salas Institute
for Hermetic Science
P.O. Box 8549
FDR Station
New York, NY 10150
U.S.A.

To request a brochure about correspondence courses or other books written by John Baines, please write to the above address or to any of the Branches that are listed in this book.

For now, I send you my best wishes for your spiritual perfection and personal excellence.

John Baines

Further information regarding the Teachings of John Baines can be obtained by contacting any of the branches listed below:

NORTH AMERICA

USA
The Dario Salas Institute
for Hermetic Science
P.O. Box 8549
FDR Station
New York, NY 10150, U.S.A.

SOUTH AMERICA

CHILE
Instituto Filosófico Hermético
World Headquarters
Casilla 14675
Santiago, Chile

COLUMBIA
Instituto Filosófico
Hermético
Apdo. 110.028
Santa Fé di Bogota,
Colombia

VENEZUELA
Instituto Filosófico
Hermético
Apdo. 75099 C. 1070-A
Caracas 1070-A
Venezuela

ARGENTINA
Fundación Instituto
Filosófico Hermético
Casilla 1426
Buenos Aires 1000,
Rep. Argentina

EUROPE

SPAIN
Instituto Filosófico Hermético
Apdo. 50600
Madrid, Spain

BULGARIA
Ars Hermetica
P.O. Box 17
1408 Sophia
Bulgaria

RUSSIAN FEDERATION
The Dario Salas Institute
P.O. Box 951
Moscow Center
Moscow 101000 , Russia

For other books by John Baines, please use the order form below:

Prices and availability subject to change without notice.

The Secret Science
__ ISBN 1-882692-01-2........................$12.95
The Stellar Man
__ ISBN 1-882692-04-7.......................$14.95
The Science of Love
__ ISBN 1-882692-00-4........................$12.95
HypsoConsciousness
__ ISBN 1-882692-02-0.......................$9.95
Morals for the 21st Century
__ ISBN 1-882692-03-9.......................$18.95

Use this page for ordering:
THE JOHN BAINES COLLECTION
P.O. Box 8556, F.D.R. Station
NYC, NY 10150
books@ihpny.org

Please send me the above title(s). I am enclosing $ ....
(Please add $3.50 per order to cover shipping and handling). Send check or money order—no cash or C.O.D.s please. New York Residents must please add 8.25% tax.

Mr/Mrs/Ms   ....

Address   ....

City/State/Zip ....

For credit card payment:
American Express/Visa/Master Card
Card Number .... Expiration Date ....
Signature   ....

Books also available at Amazon.com